THE DOCTRINE OF PROPOSITIONS
AND TERMS

The Doctrine of
Propositions and Terms

A. N. Prior

Edited by P. T. Geach and A. J. P. Kenny

Duckworth

First published in 1976 by
Gerald Duckworth & Company Limited
The Old Piano Factory
43 Gloucester Crescent, London NW1

© 1976 The Estate of A. N. Prior

ISBN 0 7156 0691 3

Printed in Great Britain
Ebenezer Baylis and Son Limited
The Trinity Press, Worcester, and London

CONTENTS

INTRODUCTION

In 1949, while he was Professor of Philosophy at the University of Canterbury in New Zealand, Arthur Prior began work on a Dictionary of Formal Logic. By July of that year he had reached the middle C's and sent a sample to the Clarendon Press in Oxford. The publishers' readers were enthusiastic about the standard of the material, but doubtful whether there would be a demand for it in dictionary form. They suggested that a textbook would be more appropriate. Prior accepted the suggestion and by the end of the year had drafted a chapter in the new style. He grew enthusiastic, and found to his own surprise that he had much that was original to say even about stock topics.

He worked on the book throughout 1950 and 1951 reading widely and writing copiously. By May he had fixed on a title, 'The Craft of Formal Logic'. The manuscript was completed on 6 December 1951 and ran to some 220,000 words. After a historical introduction, giving a brief history of logic from Aristotle to Wittgenstein's *Tractatus*, the book was divided into three parts. The first, the logic of categoricals, after a chapter on theories of the nature of the proposition, consisted principally of an analysis of Aristotle's *De Interpretatione* and *Prior Analytics*, with later developments of them, in the theory of conversion and syllogistic in traditional and early modern logis. Part Two, the Logic of Hypotheticals, began with the logic of compound propositions in Aristotle, the Stoics and Boethius, went on to discuss the dilemma, and finally introduced the reader to truth-functions and discussed the nature of material implication. Part Three was devoted to relations between the logic of hypotheticals and categoricals, with particular reference to Boole. Part Four was about the logic of terms and the logic of relations, discussing general and singular terms from Whately to Russell, existential import in Mill and Brentano, and relation in de Morgan, Peirce and Johnson. Part Five, entitled 'Modal Logic and the Logic of Logic', was the most significant from the point of view of Prior's later development. It contained two chapters, one on the relation between modality and quantity, and the other about *Principia Mathematica* and the axiomatisation of truth-functions and syllogistic. The full list of chapters of *The Craft of Formal Logic* is printed as an appendix to the present volume.

It was not surprising that the Clarendon Press did not find it easy to reach a decision about a volume of such formidable proportions. In January 1953 the publishers gave their verdict. They were willing to publish the book in principle; but they thought it needed extensive cutting, since it was too long and devoted a disproportionate amount of space to Aristotelian and medieval logic at the expense of modern logic.

Meanwhile, Prior's own interests in logic had shifted, and he had had second thoughts about the publication of the volume as it stood. He agreed to rewrite the work; but in fact, he wrote an entirely new book, which is now familiar to philosophers and logicians under the title *Formal Logic*. It was written at amazing speed: Part One, which consists of much completely new material on the propositional calculus, protothetic and quantification, was ready for despatch to the publishers by 22 March 1953; Parts Two and Three, which overlapped with, but hardly reproduced, parts of *The Craft*, were completed by May. The book was finally published in 1955.

The Craft of Formal Logic as it originally stood remained unpublished. After Prior's death in 1969 some of his friends suggested that the question of its publication should be re-opened, and Mrs Mary Prior entrusted us with the task of deciding whether, and in what form, it should be submitted to a publisher.

It was immediately clear that there could be no question at this date of publishing the original volume in its entirety. Though very few pages of the book had been simply transferred bodily into *Formal Logic*, there were substantial overlappings with that work; and it was obvious that Prior had quarried the manuscript in several places for use in articles, notably for his essay on 'The algebra of the copula' and for contributions to *The Encyclopedia of Philosophy*. Much of what he wrote on Aristotle and on medieval logic has now been rendered obsolete by the work of such writers as Ackrill, Patzig and the Kneales; all that was original in the more formal chapters had been superseded by his own later work. Some of the chapters dealt with dead wood in the traditional logic which even Prior's touch could not bring alive.

None the less, it appeared to us that when all this material had been removed there remained substantial passages of permanent interest which had not been antiquated by later work, and which made up a valuable contribution to the philosophical prehistory of contemporary logic. In this volume we present five chapters of the original *Craft*, two from the first part, and three from the fourth part. They make up a self-contained account of the traditional doctrine of propositions and terms.

Like Prior's early work *Logic and the Basis of Ethics*, the parts of *The Craft* that we now present are of an historical and critical nature; Prior is not concerned to decide for us these controverted questions of logical doctrine. He may be compared to an experienced judge summing up in a complicated civil action: the case for each side is clearly and fairly presented, and although on some issues the summing-up will from the nature of the case be tantamount to a pretty clear direction of the jury, the jurymen themselves are left to decide the issues. Prior's own final views on some of the problems are to be found in *Objects of Thought*, Chapters 1 to 4. The logic of tense, which was to occupy so much of Prior's attention later, is here barely hinted at; true to his judicial role, he merely records that Aristotle and the medieval logicians held that one and the same opinion or proposition could be now true, now false, according to changes in the world, but that later logicians rejected this view. No direction of the jury on this issue is even implied.

The value of such an historical survey is to be measured by the ill effects of ignoring our predecessors' labours. There is a saying that those who will not learn the history of philosophy are compelled to relive it. The import of this epigram may be spelled out under three heads.

First, those who ignore history are in danger of taking some theory to be new when it has already been extensively discussed, and of following a trail along what has already turned out to be a blind alley. For example, someone who knows the entangled doctrine of sentences, propositions, beliefs and facts (presented in Chapters 1 and 2 of this book) will identify the contrast between a sentence and the statement it is 'used to make' as a re-labelling of the old contrast between a sentence and the proposition 'expressed'; and the new label has the distinct disadvantage of suggesting, and inducing some people to accept, the clearly wrong view that sentences not used assertorically correspond to no 'statements' and thus cannot be regarded as true or false in their purport.

Secondly, when work already done is forgotten, needed distinctions may be obliterated and alternative solutions to problems may be overlooked. Two instances may be cited here from Prior's book; each time, the unjustly forgotten work is in Neville Keynes's *Formal Logic*. Discussions of intension vs. extension, analyticity, truth by convention, etc., suffer much from neglect of Keynes's careful distinctions (see Chapter 4, section three). And there is a widely prevalent ignorance of what alternative views are coherently tenable about the existential import of categorical propositions (see Chapter 5, section 3). One of those things which 'everybody knows' is that if empty terms are admitted, then it is not possible to have a system preserving the square of opposition, the laws of conversion and the traditionally valid syllogisms all together: as Prior remarks, they can all be easily preserved if we read affirmative categoricals as having, and negatives as not having, existential import for the subject term.

No one has devoted more ingenuity to bringing out the soundness and concrete applicability of the traditional logic than Strawson; but even Strawson does not mention this possible solution in his *Introduction to Logical Theory*. Strawson himself offers to salvage the whole of the Aristotelian tradition, and post-Aristotelian doctrines like obversion and inversion as well, by a new reading of categoricals in terms not of predicate logic but of 'presupposition'. Prior's historical account shows that earlier writers foreshadowed this doctrine (see below, pp. 125f.); it also makes clear that this reading does not really solve the problem of freely allowing empty terms within the Aristotelian framework. If Prior's simple conservative interpretation were better known, the 'presupposition' doctrine might well find less favour than it does.

Thirdly, a doctrine received as a traditional inheritance may take on quite a new look when we see how it came to be in its present form: we may then decide to reject it, and if we still hold it we shall do so with better right and clearer understanding than before. Thus, in this work Prior brings out how Russell's doctrine of existence related to previous discussions (Chapter 5, sections 2–3): it is like watching a pure and sharp-edged crystal forming itself in a turbid concentrated solution, and for someone who knows the history well

'Existence is not a predicate' will no longer be an ill-understood slogan.

These examples by no means exhaust the contemporary interest of Prior's historical topics. Whether class designations like 'the class of all men' and abstract terms like 'redness' each refer to just one object is still very much a live issue (see Chapter 4, section 4). On the first point Prior states Russell's view of classes as 'logical constructions' far more simply, clearly and plausibly than Russell did; on the second, he shows that people vainly try to disallow statements like 'redness is not a material object' by insisting on talking about material-object *words* rather than material objects; this razor is far too blunt to shave Plato's beard. Again, the disputes about whether '*Fa*' and 'not-*Fa*' are genuine contradictories (suppose there is no such thing as *a*?), which Prior considers in Chapter 5, section 4, have recently flared up again, in ways that we cannot here enter upon; Quine's discussion in *From a logical Point of View*, Chapter 9, is just one easily accessible example.

In these chapters we have chosen to present we have limited our editorial work to matters of punctuation and paragraphing, to the removal of explicit or implicit cross-references to other parts of the work, to the correction of one or two obvious slips and the removal of footnote references which are now obsolete. We are indebted to Mr John Mackie for allowing us to use his copy of the original typescript, and to Mrs Mary Prior for her encouragement at every stage of the work.

P. T. GEACH
A. J. P. KENNY

CHAPTER ONE

Propositions and Sentences

1. The proposition in Aristotle and his successors

The basic subject of Aristotle's *De Interpretatione*, in which his most detailed treatment of propositions is to be found, is affirmation and denial. It concerns the 'interpretation' of the 'Yes' or 'No' with which a man replies to a question capable of being thus answered;[1] this being an indispensable preliminary to the study of what deductions an opponent may fairly draw from such admissions or repudiations.

Aristotle appears to think of affirmation and denial primarily as functions of the spoken word, though he notes that 'spoken words are symbols of mental experience' and may in turn be 'symbolised' by being written down.[2] Neither speech nor thought, though, is exhausted by affirmation and denial, i.e. by the kind of speech or thought that is capable of truth and falsity; indeed, this kind presupposes another kind, for there can be no truth or falsehood without a 'combination' or 'separation' of elements to which these predicates are inapplicable; these elements being (in the case of speech) nouns and verbs. Thus there is no truth or falsity in the noun 'goat-stag', considered by itself; at least 'is' or 'is not' must be attached to it before we have anything to which either assent or dissent can intelligibly be given.[3] (Even 'Goat-stag is' is hardly a proposition in English; but its equivalent would pass in Greek. The English would need an article—'A goat-stag exists', 'The goat-stag is no fiction.')

That truth and falsehood, affirmation and denial, thus presuppose complexity, is also emphasised in the *Categoriae*;[4] and the idea that

---

[1] See Minto, *Logic Inductive and Deductive*, p. 4 n. 1. The most explicit reference in the *De Interpretatione* itself to the game of 'dialectic' out of which Aristotle's logic grew, is in ch. 11 (20ᵇ22–31).

[2] 16ᵃ4–5.

[3] 16ᵃ9–18.

[4] 2ᵃ4–10, and 13ᵇ10–12.

13

the combination required is of a noun and a verb goes back to Plato's *Sophist*.[1] Complexity alone, it should be noted, is not enough in Aristotle's eyes to make a form of speech a proposition (that is, an affirmation or a denial). Mere physical complexity even nouns and verbs on their own possess, being made up of sounds and syllables. But the sounds and syllables of which nouns and verbs are composed are themselves without meaning, whereas the nouns and verbs of which propositions and other sentences are composed are not without meaning (even though they are without truth or falsehood).[2] There are, indeed, 'composite nouns', such as 'pirate-boat' (*epaktrokelēs*), in which the parts contribute to the meaning of the whole; but even here, Aristotle contends, the parts are without meaning in themselves.[3] (It is easy to take such a view of the fragment *epaktro* in *epaktrokelēs*—the 'psycho-' of 'psychophysical' would be an English parallel—but Aristotle explicitly applies it to the other part, the *kelēs*, despite the fact that this, like our 'physical', *is* a word on its own too.) He also notes that the compound formed by attaching a sign of negation to a noun, e.g. the compound 'not-man', is 'not a sentence or a denial'; though it is not, strictly speaking, in his view, a noun either. 'There is indeed no recognised term by which we may denote such an expression . . . Let it then be called an indefinite noun.'[4] He decides similarly to give the name 'indefinite verb' to 'such expressions as "is not-healthy", "is not-ill" '[5] (*ouch hugiainei, ou kamnei*: Ross's translation of the latter as 'ails-not'[6] conveys the structure of these expressions more accurately).

Aristotle points out, further, that even where we have a combination of a noun and verb, definitely making up a 'sentence' (*logos, oratio*), we may still not have a 'proposition' (*logos apophantikos, enunciatio*), for of sentences, 'only such are propositions as have in them either truth or falsity', and this is not true of all. 'Thus a prayer is a sentence, but is neither true nor false.' With these non-

---

[1] 262 A–C.
[2] 16ᵃ20; 16ᵇ7, 26–33.
[3] 16ᵃ23–7, 16ᵇ34–5.
[4] 16ᵇ30 ff.
[5] 16ᵇ12–16.
[6] W. D. Ross, *Aristotle*, p. 27.

indicative sentences he has no more to do in this treatise; their investigation 'belongs rather to the study of rhetoric or of poetry'.[1]

The definitions and distinctions laid down in the *De Interpretatione* are echoed with little substantial alteration by the logicians of the Middle Ages. Says Petrus Hispanus, *Propositio est oratio verum vel falsum significans iudicando, ut 'homo currit' vel aliter: propositio est affirmatio vel negatio alicuius de aliquo*[2]—'A proposition is a sentence signifying something true or false in the manner of a judgement, such as "A man is running"; or again, a proposition is the affirming or denying something of something.' In the paragraph just before this definition, the proposition is distinguished from other *orationes* by its 'indicative' character. 'Of fully expressed sentences (*orationum perfectarum*) some are indicative, as "A man is running"; some imperative, as "Make a fire"; some optative, as "Would that I may be a good clerk", others subjunctive, as "If you should come to me, I will give you a horse". Of all these sentences only the indicative is a proposition.' Before this, again, an *oratio* or sentence is defined as a form of *vox significativa ad placitum*, utterance which has acquired meaning by convention; being distinguished from other such utterances by being 'composite' or 'complex',[3] having 'parts with independent meaning', these parts being nouns and verbs.[4] It is plain that most of this is the purest Aristotle. There is, indeed, compared with Aristotle, a certain proliferation of non-indicative sentential forms; though, by comparison with Apuleius, Peter is positively restrained at this point.[5] Also, there is some appearance of novelty in the reference to 'judgement' (*significans iudicando*) in the definition of *propositio*; but it is hardly more than an appearance. Peter's exact phrase, 'signifying in the manner of a judgement', is in the spirit of Aristotle's 'dialectical' treatment of the proposition as one of a pair of contradictory positions between which a man is invited to make his choice (*iudicare*); and a connection between statement and judgment is already plainly enough indicated in Aristotle's reference, at the beginning of the *De Interpretatione*, to

[1] 17ᵃ2–8.

[2] *Summulae Logicales*, Bochenski's edition, 1.07.

[3] 1.03.

[4] 1.06.

[5] Apuleius lists, as species of *oratio*, '*imperandi mandandi succensendi optandi vovendi irascendi odiandi invidendi favendi miserandi admirandi contemnendi obiurgandi paenitendi deplorandi*'.

speech as the symbolising of thought, and to forms of thought as well as of speech which are capable of truth and falsehood.[1]

In our English *Summulae*, the *Elements* of Archbishop Whately, the Proposition is introduced as 'Judgment expressed in words', and defined as 'a Sentence indicative (or asserting), i.e. which affirms or denies'. 'It is this that distinguishes a *Proposition* from a *Question*, a *Command*, etc.' A little later he notices the connection of the proposition with truth and falsehood, observing that 'as, on the one hand, every *Proposition* must be either true or false, so, on the other hand, *nothing else* can be, strictly speaking, true or false', though the terms are often loosely applied in other ways.[2] In an Appendix he says again that 'Truth, in the strict logical sense, applies to propositions, and to nothing else; and consists in the conformity of the declaration made to the actual state of the case.' He goes on to suggest that 'it would be an advantage if the word Trueness or Verity could be introduced and employed in this sense, since the word Truth is so often used to denote the "true" *Proposition itself.* "What I tell you is the *Truth*; the *Truth* of what I say shall be proved"; the term is here used in these two senses; *viz.* in the "concrete", and in the "abstract" sense.'[3] John Stuart Mill says, 'The answer to every question which it is possible to frame, must be contained in a Proposition, or Assertion. Whatever can be an object of belief, or even of disbelief, must, when put into words, assume the form of a proposition. All truth and all error lie in propositions. What, by a convenient misapplication of an abstract term, we call a Truth, means simply a True Proposition; and errors are false propositions.' And 'a proposition, according to the common simple definition, which is sufficient for our purpose, is *discourse, in which something is affirmed or denied of something*'.[4] In Jevons, a proposition is said to be 'any combination of words expressing an act of judgment . . . What the logician calls a proposition the grammarian calls a *sentence*. But though every proposition is a sentence . . . not . . . every sentence is a proposition.' A 'Sentence Interrogative or a Question, a Sentence Imperative or a Command, a Sentence Optative, . . . and an Exclamatory Sentence' are not propositions, at least as they

---

[1] Cf. also the *Categoriae*, 4ᵃ25–8, 37–4ᵇ2.
[2] R. Whately, *Elements of Logic*, II.ii.1.
[3] Appendix I, xxix.
[4] J. S. Mill, *System of Logic*, I.i.2.

stand; but only the 'Sentence Indicative'.[1] In the first edition of Keynes's *Formal Logic* (1884),[2] a proposition is defined as 'a sentence indicative or assertory (as distinguished, for example, from sentences imperative or exclamatory)', or 'in other words . . . a sentence making an affirmation or denial'. In the second edition (1887),[3] Keynes repeats this and adds to it, 'It is the verbal expression of a judgment'. In the fourth edition (1906), no formal definition is offered, but much is said about the question, then much agitated, as to whether the proposition or the judgement is the more proper subject of logical study, and it is said in passing that a proposition is 'a judgment expressed in language', while a judgement is 'a proposition as understood'.[4] Joseph says that 'the true unit of thought . . . is the *Judgement*, or *Proposition*: between which where a distinction is intended, it is that the proposition is the expression in words of a judgement'.[5] Again, 'A proposition is a sentence, but not merely a sentence: it is a sentence expressing or meaning a judgement'.[6] And 'to judge, in the logical sense of the word, is . . . to affirm or deny a predicate of a subject'.[7] Further, 'Every judgement makes an assertion, which must be either true or false . . . This capacity for truth or falsehood is the peculiar distinction of judgement, expressed grammatically in a proposition by the indicative mood. Imperatives, optatives, exclamations, and interrogations are not propositions as they stand.'[8]

2. *The proposition in itself*

There is the tradition. It has a consistency, and a faithfulness to its origin, which speak for themselves. All its spokesmen agree that a proposition is a form of speech, a sentence, though not any sort of sentence—it must be in the indicative mood, capable of truth or falsehood, and somehow connected with 'judgement'. But what is the exact nature of this connection with judgement? According to Whately, Jevons, Keynes and Joseph, the proposition is the (verbal)

[1] W. S. Jevons, *Elementary Lessons in Logic*, VIII.
[2] §35.
[3] §34.
[4] §46.
[5] H. W. B. Joseph, *An Introduction to Logic*, 2nd edition, p. 14.
[6] Ibid., p. 18.
[7] p. 159.
[8] p. 160.

'expression' of the judgement. The language of Petrus Hispanus, and of Mill, is a little different from this, though not necessarily inconsistent with it. According to Petrus Hispanus, the proposition 'signifies' (rather than *is*) 'something true or false'; and this something would not be the *iudicium* or judgement—it would rather be what comes up for judgement. According to Mill, similarly, the proposition 'puts into words', not a belief or disbelief, but 'whatever can be the object' of a belief or disbelief (though this putting into words of its object may be precisely what is meant, in other writers, by the 'expression' of a belief or disbelief, or of a 'judgement'). And by some writers, especially by some writers at Cambridge during the first quarter of this century, 'propositions' have been identified not merely with the sentences which 'signify' these objects of belief or judgement, but with these objects of belief or judgement themselves. Thus Johnson lists 'three notions which, though intimately connected, must be clearly distinguished: namely (1) what may be called the sentence; (2) the proposition; and (3) the judgement'; and instead of identifying the proposition with the sentence and describing it as the verbal expression of a judgement, he says that 'the sentence may be summarily defined as the verbal expression of a judgment or of a proposition'.[1] Judgement and proposition are distinguished by the former being one of a variety of possible 'attitudes of thought', and the latter (the proposition), the 'object towards which that thought may be directed',[2] a 'single entity' which is 'the same whatever may be the attitude adopted towards it'.[3]

The difference between the view which Johnson's language naturally suggests,[4] and such a view as Mill's, does not seem more than verbal. Mill does not depart from the traditional identification of the proposition with the (indicative) sentence; but he distinguishes clearly between the 'three notions' which Johnson mentions, and he insists, in particular, that no adequate account can be given either of propositions (Johnson's 'sentences') or of beliefs and disbeliefs ('judgements') unless we distinguish between 'the state of mind called Belief' and 'what is believed', between the 'fact of

[1] *Logic*, I.i.i.
[2] Ibid.
[3] I.i.3.
[4] I do not simply say 'Johnson's view', for (as we shall see) Johnson has other language which suggests another view.

entertaining' a 'doctrine or opinion', and the doctrine or opinion entertained, between 'assent' and 'what is assented to', in short, between Johnson's 'judgements' on the one hand and his 'propositions' on the other. It is to this, the 'objective' factor—'not . . . the art of believing, but . . . the thing believed'—that Mill refers throughout when he asks the series of questions, 'What is the immediate object of belief in a Proposition? What is the matter of fact signified by it? What is it to which, when I assert the proposition, I give my assent, and call upon others to give theirs? What is that which is expressed by the form of discourse called a Proposition, and the conformity of which to fact constitutes the truth of that proposition?'[1] The entity here enquired about, we may note, is (1) not a proposition in the sense of 'sentence', but is rather 'expressed' or 'signified by a proposition in this sense; (2) not a belief, but rather an 'immediate object' of belief; (3) not a fact, but rather something which may 'conform' to fact, and 'the conformity of which to fact constitutes the truth of' the proposition (sentence) which 'expresses' or 'signifies' it. (It is a 'matter of fact', though). And though not called by Mill a 'proposition', it corresponds exactly, in all these respects, to what Johnson (following Professor Moore and Lord Russell) calls by that name. And the important point philosophically is not, of course, whether such entities, if there are any, should or should not be called 'propositions', but whether there are any such entities.

That there are, was vigorously maintained, at about the time when Mill's *System of Logic* first appeared, by Bolzano. Bolzano spoke of the 'proposition in itself' or 'sentence in itself' (*Satz an sich*—the phrase is obviously an adaptation of the *Ding an sich*, 'Thing in itself', of Kant), by which he meant 'any statement whatever to the effect that something is or is not, irrespective of whether the statement be true or false, irrespective of whether any person ever formulated it in words, and even irrespective of whether it ever entered any mind as a thought'.[2] Here a proposition is admitted to be a 'statement' (*Aussage*); but a 'statement' is plainly understood neither as a stating nor as the words in which we state a thing, but as the thing stated in these words, which thing may also exist

[1] *System of Logic*, I.V.I.
[2] Quoted and translated in D. A. Steele's Historical Introduction to the English edition of Bolzano's *Paradoxes of the Infinite*, p. 45.

unstated and unthought-of. This is going rather further than Johnson, who insists (whether or not this is consistent with his other remarks on this subject) that 'the proposition is not so to speak a self-subsistent entity, but only a factor in the concrete act of judgment',[1] statements which appear to be about the 'proposition in itself' (e.g. that a certain proposition is false) being in reality statements about *any* assertion of that proposition (e.g. that any assertion of it is erroneous). Johnson seems to go at least part of the way towards Bolzano's position when he says that a proposition coincides 'not exactly with what *has been* asserted, but with what is in its nature assertible'.[2]

Another Continental variant of the theory of 'propositions in themselves' is Meinong's theory of 'objectives'. These, like the 'propositions' of Russell, Moore and Johnson, are the objects before our mind in such activities as judging and supposing; they are the objective entities denoted or meant by sentences, in contrast with the mental states 'expressed' by them. But they differ from propositions, at all events as the latter are understood by Johnson, and from the unnamed entities of Mill, in their relation to fact. Johnson's 'propositions', and the entities enquired after by Mill, accord with facts if they are true and discord with them if they are not, and in either case are distinct from them. But in Meinong 'factuality', or 'being the case', is simply a property which belongs to some of his 'objectives' and not to others, so that some of them, e.g. that $7 + 5 = 12$, simply are facts, and others, e.g. that $7 + 5 = 2$, are not. On a theory like Johnson's, this example would involve not merely two entities, a factual objective and an unfactual one, but three, namely the fact that $7 + 5 = 12$, the 'proposition' that $7 + 5 = 12$, which accords with this fact, and so is true, and the 'proposition' that $7 + 5 = 2$, which discords with the fact, and so is false.[3] On neither view, we may note, is there any such entity as 'the fact that $7 + 5 = 2$'. Whether or not there are 'unfactual objectives' or 'false propositions', there could hardly be false or unfactual facts; though we shall find that those who dislike 'proposi-

[1] *Logic*, I.i.I.

[2] Ibid. On the point of Johnson's consistency or otherwise, see C. D. Broad, *Examination of McTaggart's Philosophy*, vol. 1, pp. 69–70.

[3] See J. N. Findlay, *Meinong's Theory of Objects*, ch. 3, section ix, for a full discussion of the relation of Meinong's theory to this one.

tions in themselves' have sometimes been pressed into talking as if there were.

The most complete marshalling of the arguments for and against *Sätze an sich* is probably that in Professor Ryle's Aristotelian Society paper entitled *Are There Propositions?*[1] This contains, first, a very full statement, in four sections, of the arguments in their favour, followed by a brief summary of the precise position which these arguments appear to establish; then a rather more cursory statement of the arguments against them; and finally, a careful statement of an alternative theory, with some attempt to show how this theory really does provide an alternative solution to the problems for which the theory of *Sätze an sich* was devised. After the publication of this paper, Mr Richard Robinson, at that time a disciple of Cook Wilson, complained (in a note in *Mind*,[2] to which Professor Ryle subsequently replied[3]) that the concluding portion of its task was unsatisfactorily performed. Other useful items for the student, from the very copious literature that exists on this subject, are the chapter on 'Truth and Falsehood' in Lord Russell's *Problems of Philosophy*,[4] written after he had himself ceased to believe in 'propositions in themselves', and principally devoted to the exposition of an alternative theory; also the chapter on 'Propositions' in Professor Broad's *Examination of McTaggart's Philosophy*,[5] where the considerations that have led to the belief in 'propositions in themselves' are set forth, and an attempt made to assess their weight, and to meet them in an alternative way.

The first of the favourable arguments listed by Professor Ryle is that from what has been called the 'intentionality' of all forms of consciousness.[6] This is a medieval way of speaking which has passed into modern jargon through Brentano. *Intentio*, in the later medieval writers, meant the direction of thought or speech towards that which is thought or spoken of; and Brentano, in a famous passage in his *Psychology*, says that the distinguishing feature of a 'psychical phenomenon' is 'what the medieval Schoolmen called "intentional

---

[1] *Proc. Arist. Soc.*, 1929–30, pp. 91–126.
[2] R. Robinson, 'Mr. Ryle on Propositions', *Mind* 1931, pp. 73–8.
[3] G. Ryle, 'Mr. Ryle on Propositions (Rejoinder)', *Mind* 1931, pp. 330–4.
[4] Ch. 12, esp. pp. 124–30.
[5] Vol. 1, ch. 4.
[6] *Proc. Arist. Soc.* 1929–30, pp. 92–5. Cf. Broad, op. cit., pp. 68–70.

inexistence" . . . and what we ourselves may call . . . reference to a content, direction towards an object (without necessarily meaning by that a reality), or "immanent objectivity". Every psychical phenomenon contains something in itself as its object, each in its own manner. In representation, there is something represented, in judgment something that is admitted or repudiated, in love something that is loved, in hate something that is hated, in desire something that is desired, and so for the rest.'[1] All forms of consciousness have, to use Professor Ryle's word, their 'accusatives'; it is of the nature of every *cogitatio* to have a *cogitatum*, and so, specifically, of every *iudicatio* or judgement to have a *iudicatum*. Both Professor Ryle and Professor Broad point out that even if, as this line of thought suggests, it is inconceivable that a mental act should be without an object distinct from itself, the object might still be quite inseparable from the act and incapable of existing apart from it. This, indeed, Brentano himself saw, and was at first inclined to think that the objects of consciousness are not 'mind-independent'.[2] (Johnson, as we have seen, sometimes seems to speak in the same strain.)

The main considerations which have suggested that 'propositions' or 'objectives' are more than merely 'immanent' objects are the following: (a) The entities, whatever they are, that constitute what we believe and disbelieve, and what we 'mean' by the sentences we write and utter—what we 'state' in our statements—seem to have numerous characteristic properties and mutual relations which attach to them quite regardless of whether or not they are actually being believed or stated by anyone. Thus propositions seem to be and remain true or false (as the case may be), quite regardless of whether or not anyone is stating or believing or even disbelieving or merely supposing them. Again, that one proposition is or is not a logical consequence of another, and that one proposition is or is not logically inconsistent with another, seem to be facts about the propositions in question which have nothing to do with their being thought or stated. (b) It often seems necessary to speak of different people as 'believing the same thing', or of the same person as 'believing the same thing' at different times, or of some people as believing and others as disbelieving some one thing (there could be no real conflict of opinion unless there were this), or of the same person as at one

[1] F. Brentano, *Psychologie vom empirischen Standpunkt* (1874), II.i.5.
[2] Ibid.

time believing and at another time disbelieving some one thing. Different judgements may be, as Professor Broad puts it, 'co-referential'. There is an analogous fact in the case of sentences. We often say that different sentences, including sentences in different languages, have the same meaning, i.e. mean the same thing. All this suggests that the objects of our beliefs, and meanings of our sentences, are 'public', 'neutral' entities independent of those beliefs and sentences.

But must these public and neutral objects of our believing be these ghostly 'propositions in themselves'? Could they not be public and neutral entities of a more or less familiar sort? Might they not be simply *things*, or as philosophers say, 'substances'? The mere grammar of the word 'believe' is quite against this suggestion. We do, indeed, say sometimes that we 'believe Mr So-and-so', but this does not mean that Mr So-and-so is the object of our believing as he is the object of our seeing when we see him. 'I believe Mr So-and-so' means 'I believe what he says', and concretely this must always amount to 'I believe that something or other (whatever it is that Mr So-and-so says) is the case.' Again, we say 'I believe in God'; but this means 'I believe that God exists.' Then we speak, as has been observed above, of different people believing 'the same thing'; but if we ask what the 'thing' is that they all believe, the answer will always be a 'that . . .' clause ('that God exists', say), and we do not name or describe 'substances' in this way. And anyway, it is nonsense to talk of 'substances' as being true or false, or as following from or being inconsistent with other substances. (So— on the matter of inconsistency—Professor Ryle;[1] though a little later[2] he says that the proposition theory is precisely the theory that propositions are 'substances', in the very broad sense of entities which 'have qualities and relations and possess their status and their characters independently of other entities'. 'In consequence', on this theory, 'the sentences, "Honesty is the worst policy" and "Honesty is the best policy" are *names* of two different substances of which one has the quality of being false, the other that of being true.')

Another alternative to 'propositions' as the objects of believing and disbelieving, would be *facts*. This suggestion does meet the

[1] Op. cit., p. 103.
[2] p. 105.

'grammatical' objection outlined above; for facts too are named or described by 'that . . .' clauses—we say not only 'I believe that God exists', but also 'It is a fact that God exists', or 'That God exists is a fact'. Meinong, as we have seen, does identify at least some of his 'objectives' with facts. But even when we confine our attention to the most favourable case, that of the objects of beliefs that are true, there are difficulties about the identification of these objects with facts. For one thing, even if we do not make as much of it as Cook Wilson did, we must admit that there is a difference between true belief and knowledge (to use an example of Lord Russell's, a man may believe it is 6 o'clock because he sees that time on a clock which he has not noticed has stopped, and it may in fact be 6 o'clock when he looks; but one would not say that such a man 'knew' what the time was); and it seems likely that the difference between the two is that in knowledge we are directly acquainted with the fact that we know, while the immediate object of true belief is not this but something else.[1] Again, that which we believe when our belief is true is surely identical with that which we 'mean' or state by the corresponding true statement; but it is possible to understand a true statement, i.e. to know its meaning, without knowing that it is true, i.e. without knowing the fact that makes it true.[2]

In any case that which we believe when our belief is false, and state when our statement is false, cannot be a fact, for there are no false facts (and as a corollary to this, there can be no inconsistent or incompatible facts, for 'incompatibility must disqualify at least one of the incompatibles from being a fact').[3] How very difficult it is to avoid the 'proposition theory' when dealing with the meaning of false statements, is illustrated by the pitiful shifts to which Mr Robinson—one of the theory's most hard-hitting opponents—is driven when he comes to this point. 'The meaning of a true statement,' Mr Robinson tells us, 'is the fact that it states; and the meaning of a false statement is the fact that it would state if, being the same statement, it were nevertheless true.' 'The reason why we are inclined to object to this' (Mr Robinson continues) 'is that we tend to feel that what is meant by any statement must be something that is real; and since the fact meant by a false statement cannot be real,

[1] Cf. Broad, op. cit., p. 63.
[2] See Ryle, op. cit., pp. 101, 111.
[3] Ibid., p. 103.

there being no such fact, we feel that a false statement must mean not a fact but a proposition; for whereas there cannot be a real false fact, there can be a real false proposition. The cure for this state of mind is simply to realise the error of the assumption that that which is meant by any statement must be something that is real. Every statement means a fact . . . but only in the case of true statements does the fact meant exist.' Professor Ryle, in his rejoinder, uses a concrete example to bring out the 'wrong-headedness' of all this. 'I state "Bristol is bigger than London". My statement then means the fact of Bristol being bigger than London. "Oh, but it is only an unreal or non-existent fact." Then it both is and is not a fact that Bristol is bigger than London'—Mr Robinson himself having derived the 'unreality' of the 'fact meant by a false statement' from the fact that 'there is no such fact'. 'Could there be a more patent contradiction than to speak of facts which do not exist as distinguished from facts which do?'

This is, of course, precisely the contradiction from which the proposition theory is designed to save us. But do we really gain so much by substituting for an 'unreal fact', as what is believed in a false belief, an 'unfactual reality' of the same general order as facts? As Lord Russell has said, explaining his own abandonment of the proposition theory, it is 'in itself almost incredible' that there should 'be in the world entities, not dependent on the existence of judgments, which can be described as objective falsehoods . . . We feel that there could be no falsehood if there were no minds to make mistakes.'[1] The very defenders of the theory seem to have an irresistible tendency to whittle away either the unfactuality or the reality of these supposed objects of false beliefs. Thus Meinong slips into talking of unfactual objectives as if they were not and could not be, after all, *completely* unfactual. To be an 'objective' or 'objective circumstance' at all (he says in effect), that which we believe, disbelieve, suppose, etc. must have *some* sort of 'factuality', even if it is only of a 'watered-down' kind; the difference between this and the 'full-strength' factuality of facts in the ordinary sense (the difference, e.g. between the factuality of the circumstance that Caesar died in his bed and the factuality of the circumstance that Caesar was murdered) consisting in the absence in the one case, and the presence in the other, of a mysterious factor called the 'modal

[1] *Philosophical Essays*, p. 170. Cf. also *The Problems of Philosophy*, p. 124.

moment'.[1] On the other hand, exponents of the 'proposition theory', notably Johnson, seem sometimes to be contending that the object of belief, etc. is what Joseph (criticising the theory) calls a *Zwischending* ('between-thing')—'not an act of the mind, and not a real which, or the nature of which, we may come to know, but something between the two'.[2] These *Zwischendinge*, Joseph says again,[3] are 'objects of thought which are not real, but yet may be objects to all of us'. That is, they have what medieval writers called 'objective' being, i.e. they stand in the relation of 'being an object' (being thought or thought of), but do not have what the same writers called 'formal' being, i.e. 'being' *simpliciter* ('objective reality' in the present-day sense of that phrase).[4]

But not only is the conception of 'objective falsehoods' difficult; it is also doubtful whether it does, after all, explain what it sets out to explain—the objective reference of false belief. For surely error consists in some sort of misapprehension of fact, not in the quite successful apprehension of something quite different. And there is a similar objection to the form of the theory that distinguishes even the objects of true beliefs from facts. For surely the difference between true belief and knowledge consists in a different relation to the facts which are the objects of both; the difference seems misrepresented when knowledge is described as knowledge of facts, and true belief, in effect, as knowledge of (or acquaintance with) something else.[5]

3. *The ascription theory of believing*
The weakest part of the argument for the 'proposition theory' seems to be the last. We may take it as sufficiently established that belief and unbelief and similar mental attitudes are directed towards objects distinct from themselves, and also that these objects include at least some that are 'public', 'neutral', 'mind-independent'; what is much less certain is that to find these objects we must go beyond

[1] J. N. Findlay, op. cit., pp. 103 ff.

[2] H. W. B. Joseph, 'What does Mr. W. E. Johnson Mean by a Proposition?', *Mind* 1927, p. 452.

[3] Ibid., p. 453.

[4] The distinction comes from Aristotle, who argues in the *De Sophisticis Elenchis* (121ª20–6, ᵇ1–4) that 'being an object of opinion' does not entail 'being' *simpliciter*.

[5] Cf. Ryle, *Are There Propositions?*, pp. 108, 110.

'things', with their characters and mutual relations, and the 'facts' of their having these characters and relations. It is true that the 'that . . .' clauses which form the *grammatical* objects of such verbs as 'believe', 'suppose', etc., cannot denote 'things' and at least in many cases do not denote facts either; but it may be that one of the differences between believing, supposing, etc. on the one hand, and such acts as seeing, hearing, etc., on the other, is not that they have different objects but that they 'have objects' in different ways. This avenue of escape from the 'proposition theory' is at all events worth exploring.

It will be instructive at this point to examine more closely the form which the 'doctrine of intentionality' takes in John Stuart Mill. Some of Mill's utterances, as we have already seen, only seem to make sense on the 'proposition theory'; but his detailed polemic is nearly all a defence, not of the objectivity of 'what we believe', but rather of the objectivity of what our beliefs are *about*, and in almost every case these do not even look like 'propositions in themselves' but are simply 'things' or 'substances'.[1] Thus in discussing Hobbes's contention that names are 'signs of our conceptions' and 'not signs of the things themselves', Mill argues that 'names are not intended only to make the hearer conceive what we conceive, but to inform him what we believe', and 'when I use a name for the purpose of expressing a belief, it is a belief concerning the thing itself, not concerning my idea of it. When I say, "the sun is the cause of day", I do not mean that my idea of the sun causes or excites in me the idea of day; or in other words, that thinking of the sun makes me think of day. I mean, that a certain physical fact . . . causes another physical fact.'[2] Again, discussing the view that judgement consists in a putting together of 'ideas', and that the business of 'propositions' (sentences) is to 'express judgments' in this sense, Mill insists that 'propositions (except sometimes when the mind is the subject treated of) are not assertions respecting our ideas of things, but assertions respecting the things themselves. In order to believe that gold is yellow, I must, indeed, have the idea of gold, and the idea of

[1] In a somewhat different connection, Mill does mention propositions 'about' other propositions, noting that 'like other things, a proposition has attributes which may be predicated of it', as when we say that one proposition is inferable from another (*System of Logic*, i.iv.3); but there is no reason to believe that he means anything by a 'proposition' in this context beyond what he elsewhere defines a proposition as being—a declaratory sentence.

[2] *System of Logic*, i.ii.i.

yellow, and something having reference to those ideas must take place in my mind; but my belief has not reference to the ideas, it has reference to the things ... When I mean to assert anything respecting the ideas, I give them their proper name; I call them ideas; as when I say that a child's idea of a battle is unlike the reality, or that the ideas entertained of the Deity have a great effect on the characters of mankind.'[1] This last is an important argument for 'intentionality'—nothing could make the distinction between mental acts and their objects more obvious than the simple fact that mental acts sometimes *are* the objects to which mental acts are directed, and that we can clearly mark off this case from others. But it is all the time the reference of our beliefs to 'things'—to the sun, or to the substance gold—that Mill is contending for; not their reference to entities denoted by 'that ...' clauses.

In explaining the exact sense in which the thing that a belief is about may be called the 'object' of that belief, it seems natural to employ the grammatical distinction between 'direct' and 'indirect' objects, and to say that, whatever difficulty we may have in identifying the 'accusatives' of believing, etc., at least their 'datives' (or 'ablatives') are entities of a perfectly familiar sort. What about the 'accusatives' or 'direct' objects, though? Do we not still need 'propositions' for them? Meinong argued that we do, holding that 'every judgement or assumption has at least *two* objects', these being 'the objective itself and the objectum', i.e. thing, 'which the objective concerns'.[2] It may be observed, however, that if the latter is treated as a literal indirect object, the form of speech 'A believes that X is Y', or at all events the grammarian's usual way of dealing with this form, must be regarded as somewhat misleading. For the grammarian will not call X here the indirect object of 'believes', but rather the *subject* of 'is Y'. What we want is some form of statement analogous to 'A gives B to C'; and in fact we have such a form in 'A *ascribes* Y-ness to X', or 'A *attributes* Y-ness to X' (e.g. 'Othello believes that Desdemona is unfaithful' could be re-stated as 'Othello attributes unfaithfulness to Desdemona'). Here the direct object, the 'accusative', is that which appears in the other form as the *predicate* of the subordinate clause; this is what is affirmed or denied,

---

[1] Ibid., I.v.I. Cf. Keynes, *Studies and Exercises in Formal Logic*, 4th ed., §49; Johnson's *Logic*, I.x.3.

[2] J. N. Findlay, op. cit., p. 67.

'predicated', and what it is affirmed or denied of is the subject of that subordinate clause. But the subordinate clause itself, with its suggestion that the object of believing is a 'proposition', is no longer present in the new version; and if 'A believes that X is Y' is just a turn of speech for 'A attributes Y-ness to X', we have no more reason for regarding 'that X is Y' as the name of a single entity, than we have for regarding 'B to C' as the name of a single entity in 'A gives B to C'. Believing or judging, on this theory, is not the sort of relation that can hold between two terms only, represented grammatically by a subject and an object; it is rather the sort of relation that knits together three terms, represented grammatically by a subject, a direct object and an indirect one. Just as giving involves not merely a giver, and a gift, but a giver, a gift and a recipient, so judgement involves an ascriber, an ascribed character, and an object to which the character is ascribed. There is no such thing as *the* object of a belief or judgement (as the 'proposition theory' assumes that there is), not because there can be belief or judgement without any object at all, but because a belief or judgement has not one object but two.

This theory is not, as to its substance, at all new. The traditional definition of both judgement and statement, not as 'affirming or denying something', but as 'affirming or denying one thing of another', plainly suggests that what is being defined is not a two-termed but a three-termed relation. Moreover, the passage in Plato's *Sophist* from which Aristotle derived this definition is an explicit attempt to overcome the deficiencies of a theory (stated and dismissed in the dialogue to which the *Sophist* is a sequel, the *Theaetetus*) very like the 'proposition theory'. (According to this rejected theory, false opinion consists in 'opining what does not exist', *to mē on doxazein*. Compare this with Mr Robinson's description of false statement as the statement of an 'unreal fact'.) But in these early versions of the three-termed-relation theory of judgement, three-termed relations are not mentioned as such; and in fact the general notion of many-termed relations seems to have been formed only in relatively recent times (to be precise, by about 1870), and the suggestion that believing and disbelieving are instances of such relations seems to have come first from Lord Russell, who adopted this view in the period immediately after his abandonment of the 'proposition theory'.

In the works in which he advocates the theory now being considered,[1] Lord Russell does not say that 'that . . .' clauses never name single objects, but insists, on the contrary, that 'that X is Y' does name such an object if the belief that X is Y happens to be true, i.e. if the Y-ness of X, or that X is Y, is a fact; and he holds that this fact may be the direct object of a 'perception'. What he denies is that the fact that X is Y (when there is such a fact) is either the direct or the indirect object of a mere belief, even a true one; not the whole fact, but only its 'constituents', are the (direct and indirect) objects in believing. We perceive the Y-ness of X, or the fact that X is Y: but we do not believe either of these things—we do not 'believe the fact' that X is Y, or 'believe (the Y-ness of X)'; rather we 'believe (Y-ness) of (X)'; and this, of course, we can do even if there is no such fact as 'the Y-ness of X'—we can do it so long as there is such an object as X and such a character as Y-ness. 'It is,' Lord Russell[2] surmises, 'the severalness of the objects in judgment (as opposed to perception) which has led people to speak of thought as "discursive" '—a suggestion that is borne out by Plato's insistence, in the passage in the *Sophist* mentioned earlier, on the complexity of 'discourse' (*legein*), in which there must be both a noun and a verb, by comparison with mere 'naming'.

At a later period Lord Russell abandoned this 'ascription' or 'multiple relation' theory in favour of a rather different alternative to his original Bolzanesque 'proposition theory'. The multiple relation theory had the disadvantage—as he came, in his new mood, to regard it—of presupposing the existence of a Self as one of the terms of the relation.[3] It also presupposed—though his formulation of it did not make this as clear as the original Platonic formulation

---

[1] *Philosophical Essays* (1910), pp. 177 ff.; *Principia Mathematica*, Introduction to the First Edition (1910), vol. 1, pp. 43–4; *Problems of Philosophy* (1912), pp. 204 ff.; *Our Knowledge of the External World* (1914), p. 58. Lord Russell argues that believing sometimes has not only three terms but more; holding that when, say, Othello believes that Desdemona loves Cassio, this believing knits together the *four* terms Othello, Desdemona, loving and Cassio. This refinement of the theory need not be discussed here.

[2] Or Whitehead—the remark is in *Principia Mathematica*, vol. 1, p. 44.

[3] He raises this objection to it in his paper *On Propositions: What they are and How they Mean* in the Aristotelian Society Supplementary Volume II (1919), p. 27. His third theory is developed in this paper and in *The Analysis of Mind*, ch. 13.

did—the existence of Real Qualities and Real Relations (entities like 'unfaithfulness', which the believing Self called Othello might 'ascribe' to the object Desdemona); and some have found these as difficult to accept as Real Propositions. In Lord Russell's third theory, 'propositions' reappear, but in a relatively innocuous form— not as mind-independent entities, but as either sentences or (in certain fairly simple cases) groups of mental images. The organism uses propositions to refer to realities outside themselves, and the realities to which propositions thus refer are facts. Facts, Lord Russell says, are the 'objectives' of propositions. There are not, however, as on Meinong's theory, other 'objectives' beside those that are facts; the problem of the objective reference of false propositions being solved by saying that these refer to facts too, but in a different way from true ones. True propositions point towards facts, and false propositions away from them. Joseph[1] objects that to say this 'is *se payer des mots*; for what is pointing from the objective "that the sun moves" except pointing falsely towards it?' But this is a misrepresentation; for on the view which Joseph imagines he is criticising, the false proposition that the sun moves (assuming for the sake of argument that it *is* false) does not point either towards or away from 'the objective "that the sun moves" ', for there is no such objective. What makes the proposition false is its 'pointing away from' the objective (fact) 'that the sun does *not* move'.[2] A better simile might perhaps have been to say that every proposition 'approaches' some fact ('proposes' to it), and is either 'accepted' or 'rejected' by it.

A more substantial objection to either simile is that it does not seem to solve the problem of the 'meaning' of false propositions; for we can know the meaning of a false proposition without knowing that it is false, but we cannot know the fact that makes it false without knowing that it is false. The two similes do, nevertheless, bring out the fact that the meaning of a proposition is that which determines *what* fact will verify or falsify it (what fact it 'approaches'),

[1] *Mind* 1928, p. 22.

[2] Lord Russell makes this perfectly clear in the very passage to which Joseph refers. 'You may believe the proposition "To-day is Tuesday" both when in fact to-day is Tuesday, and when to-day is not Tuesday. If to-day is not Tuesday, this fact is the objective of your belief that to-day is Tuesday', though 'obviously the relation of your belief to the fact is different from what it is in the case when to-day is Tuesday' (*Analysis of Mind*, p. 272).

and in a sense also determines which of these two it will do (for
whether a proposition is true or false depends on (1) what it says,
and (2) whether the fact to which it points is as it says it is); and there
is something to be said for regarding this as the *meaning* of 'meaning'.
That is, the 'meaning' of a proposition may be defined as whatever
it is about it (it may be a different sort of thing with different sorts
of propositions) which performs these functions. We can understand
what 'The sun moves' means even if in fact it does not; and we can
understand what 'The sun moves' means without knowing the fact
that it does not (i.e. without knowing the fact which is, in Lord
Russell's language, its 'objective'); but we cannot be said to understand what 'The sun moves' means if we do not know that what
makes it true or false is the fact (whatever it is) as to whether the
sun moves or not, and that there is such a fact. Thus even error
involves a measure of knowledge—not knowledge of the fact that
makes our error error (for if we knew this, we would not err), yet
knowledge sufficient to identify this fact—knowledge of what area,
so to speak, of the realm of fact, is the area we are representing-or-
misrepresenting. This point was much insisted upon by one of the
first critics of Lord Russell's 'ascription' theory, G. F. Stout,[1] but
it is really implicit in that theory itself. For we cannot ascribe the
character P to the object S, and know what we are doing, without
knowing that there is a character P and an object S, and that their
actual relation, whatever it is, is the fact that will verify or falsify
our ascription.

4. *Proposition-types and proposition-instances*
Lord Russell tells us that the figure employed in his third theory,
of propositions as 'pointing towards' facts or 'pointing away' from
them, was suggested to him by Ludwig Wittgenstein.[2] In Wittgenstein's own work also, the *Tractatus Logico-Philosophicus*, propositions appear as symbols rather than as self-subsistent entities,
and this is now the usual way of considering them. But the *Tractatus*
raises a more subtle question than that as to what a proposition 'is',

---

[1] *Studies in Philosophy and Psychology*, XII, XIII, XV. See also Johnson, 'The
Analysis of Thinking', *Mind* 1918, pp. 140–1; and Broad, *Examination of
McTaggart's Philosophy*, vol. 1, pp. 72–6. Stout's point of view owes much to
Cook Wilson.
[2] *Analysis of Mind*, p. 272 n.

namely the question as to how we should use the phrase 'the same proposition'.

We may approach this question (though this is not quite the approach of the *Tractatus*) by asking whether the treatment of a proposition as a kind of *sentence*—that is, the traditional treatment of it and the modern too, now that the temporary vogue of the theory of Bolzano is over—entails our using the phrase 'the same proposition' in exactly the same way as we use the phrase 'the same sentence'. In actual fact our use of both these phrases, and of 'the same statement', is somewhat fluctuating, and requires elucidation. Would we say, for example, that 'John is smoking his pipe' is 'the same proposition' as '*Jean fume sa pipe*', or that they are 'different propositions with the same meaning'? Is 'He is wise', said of Plato, a different proposition from 'He is wise', said of Socrates, or is this an assignment, on different occasions, of different meanings to the same proposition? And if it is not, on the two occasions, 'the same proposition', is it nevertheless 'the same sentence'? (And if not, what is 'it'?)

Most difficulties about 'same' and 'different'—and this one is no exception—arise out of an ambiguity to which Aristotle draws attention in the *Topics*,[1] namely that between 'numerical' identity or difference (identity or difference *in numero*) and identity or difference in kind (*in specie*). 'Blue Boy won the main race on the 19th. The same animal won the main race on the 24th.' Here the identity asserted is 'numerical'; the same individual being is said to have won the two races. 'Blue Boy is a greyhound. The same animal was used for racing by the ancient Persians.' Here the identity asserted is 'specific'; it is not meant that Blue Boy was used for racing by the ancient Persians, but that animals of the same kind (greyhounds) were. Aristotle makes a further distinction between 'specific' and 'generic' identity (identity *in genere*), this difference being only one of degree. 'The same animal was used for racing by the ancient Persians' might mean, as just suggested, that they raced greyhounds; but it might mean merely ('generic' identity) that they raced dogs. And more generally, we may make many different assertions of 'identity in kind' about the same individual; for the same individual may be ranged with others in many different ways.

When we say, then, that P is the same proposition as Q, a

[1] Book I, ch. 7.

2

proposition being a piece of writing or talking, do we mean that P is the same individual piece of writing or talking as Q, or merely that P and Q are pieces of writing or talking of the same kind? And if the latter, what must individual pieces of writing or talking have in common for one to be 'the same proposition' as another? Before attempting to answer these questions, we should perhaps ask, and attempt to answer, another, namely, What constitutes an individual piece of writing or talking? Offhand, I think most people would be disposed to say that while 'John is smoking his pipe' and '*Jean fume sa pipe*' are at most the same in kind, 'John is smoking his pipe' and 'John is smoking his pipe' are numerically the same proposition or sentence. But are they?

'A common mode of estimating the amount of matter in an MS. or printed page,' says C. S. Peirce in a paragraph that has now become a standard reference,[1] 'is to count the number of words. There will ordinarily be about twenty *the*'s on a page, and of course they count as twenty words. In another sense of the word "word", however, there is but one word "the" in the English language; and it is impossible that this word should lie visibly on a page or be heard in any voice, for the reason that it is not a Single thing or a Single event. It does not exist; it only determines things that do exist. Such a definitely significant Form, I propose to term a *Type*. A Single event which happens once and whose identity is limited to that one happening or a Single object or thing which is in some single place at any one instant of time, such event or thing being significant only as occurring just when and where it does, I will venture to call a *Token* ... In order that a Type may be used, it has to be embodied in a Token which shall be a sign of the Type, and thereby of the object the Type signifies. I propose to call such a Token of a Type an *Instance* of the Type. Thus, there may be twenty Instances of the Type "the" on a page.' This distinction plainly applies to whole sentences as well as to isolated words. Thus we may say that 'John is smoking his pipe' and 'John is smoking his pipe' are numerically different 'sentence-tokens', though they are instances of the same 'sentence-type'; that is, in Aristotelian terminology, they are sentences of the same species, and so in that sense 'the same sentence'. And as far as 'propositions' are concerned, we may say at once that the dominant tendency in Logic is for the term 'pro-

[1] *Collected Papers of C. S. Peirce*, 4.537.

position' to be used not for a 'sentence-token' but for a 'sentence-type'. Not many logicians would hesitate, for example, to say that 'All men are mortal' is 'the same proposition' as 'All men are mortal', though we have here two different 'tokens'. This point is sometimes made by saying that the logician generally considers propositions in complete abstraction from who utters them or when or where they are uttered. Nor is he generally interested in the difference between 'All men are mortal' spoken and 'All men are mortal' written, or for that matter between either of these and 'All men are mortal' semaphored or signalled in Morse. These are all, to the logician, 'the same proposition'. They would also, I think, be described by most people, in most contexts, as 'the same sentence'. But there are cases where logicians would be inclined to say that 'the same proposition' was being uttered (or spoken, or signalled), though we would not be inclined to say that it was 'the same sentence'; and this is perhaps the truth behind the contention of exponents of the 'proposition theory' that the same proposition may often be 'expressed' by different sentences. This language suggests that there is a single non-verbal object of which the sentences are different names; but even if this suggestion is rejected, it may still be admitted that the sentence-tokens which are instances of a single 'proposition-type' may include ones which are instances of a number of different 'sentence-types'. An example of this might be the case first mentioned— 'John is smoking his pipe' and '*Jean fume sa pipe*'. Though there would not be unanimity about it, I think most logicians would call these two sentences 'the same proposition'. Again, logicians often say things like this: 'The logical structure of the proposition "All who love virtue love angling" is brought out more clearly by rendering it "Every lover of virtue is a lover of angling" '—language which plainly suggests that 'All who love virtue love angling' and 'Every lover of virtue is a lover of angling' are just two different 'renderings' of 'the same proposition'; though they are certainly different sentences.

What, then, must sentence-tokens have in common to be instances of 'the same sentence' and what to be instances of 'the same proposition'? Both the technical usages of logicians and grammarians, and the usages of ordinary speech, are apt to vary in different contexts, and all the different usages are complicated; but one may say broadly that a common physical form is more important for the identification of a sentence-type, and a common meaning more important for the identification of a proposition-type. All instances of 'the sentence "All lovers of virtue love angling" ' consist either of a certain fairly fixed series of sounds (though there are differences in pronunciation from one person to another which do not make the thing pronounced a different sentence), or of a certain series of marks or other signs correlated with these sounds by certain rules. On the other hand, quite a different series of sounds or marks might count as 'the same proposition' if the series had the same meaning (as in the case of 'John is smoking his pipe' and '*Jean fume sa pipe*'). Some writers carry this emphasis so far as to define a proposition without referring to classes of sentence-tokens at all, but only to classes of 'judgement-tokens'. To speak of 'the proposition "X is Y" ' is on this view a way of speaking, not about all sentence-tokens with a certain meaning, but about all judgements (i.e. individual acts of judging) with a certain objective import.[1] This would make the difference between a 'judgement' and a 'proposition' simply that between a certain kind of mental 'token' and the corresponding 'type'. Many contemporary philosophers, however,[2] deny that there are 'mental acts' (such as judging) in addition to acts of speech and writing and signalling, and would define 'the judgement that X is Y' as simply a disposition or readiness to *say* (or write, or signal) that X is Y, given the occasion (it is, we might say, a disposition to answer 'Yes' to the question 'Is it the case that X is Y?'). On this view the distinction between a judgement and a proposition is simply that between a disposition to act in a certain way and the corresponding act, and the difference between 'tokens' and 'type' appears equally in both.

But, granted that two sentence-tokens are not to be counted as instances of 'the same proposition' unless they have the same meaning, what are we to say that the word 'meaning' means when we speak of the 'meaning' of a sentence-token? Some modern logicians, following Wittgenstein, argue that two sentences have the same meaning, and are consequently instances of the same proposition, if they have the same 'truth-conditions', i.e. if any possible circumstances which would make either of them true or false would have

[1] So, e.g., C. D. Broad, *Examination of McTaggart's Philosophy*, vol. 1, ch. 4, 2.1.

[2] Most notably Professor Ryle, in *The Concept of Mind*.

the same effect on the other. On this view, we would need to say, for example, that 'It is raining' is the same proposition as 'Either it is raining but not snowing or it is doing both', for any possible state of affairs in which the former is true is one in which the latter is, and *vice versa*, and similarly with falsity. (If it is doing both, both the simple and the compound proposition are true; if it is raining but not snowing, both are true; if it is snowing but not raining, both are false; and if it is doing neither, both are false.) Objections to this are (a) that it seems to involve 'propositions in themselves' (as well as the propositions that are sentences), under the guise of 'possible states of affairs'; and (b) that the suggested usage would make it always false to say that two different propositions logically imply one another, since by the criterion suggested, this relation would automatically make any such allegedly different propositions the same proposition. (For if each implies the other, any circumstance under which either would be true, would be one under which the other would be.) It might be possible to meet the first objection by some further analysis of 'possible circumstance' or 'possible state of affairs'; at all events, it is the second objection which most directly concerns the formal logician, who is, I think, bound—if he is to pursue his own subject without intolerable awkwardness—to add to the suggested condition the further one that for two sentence-tokens to be (instances of) 'the same proposition', they must have the same logical form. The elucidation of the concept of 'logical form' cannot be undertaken at this stage; but two sentences are certainly different in logical form, though they need not differ in logical force, if one is simple (like 'It is raining') and the other compound (like 'Either it is raining but not snowing or it is doing both').

Tokens, then, which are not 'the same sentence' may nevertheless be 'the same proposition', and we may express this fact, if we wish to, by saying that 'the same proposition may be expressed by different sentences'. Modern logicians would generally add that the converse is also true, i.e. that different propositions may sometimes be expressed by the same sentence. This occurs when sentence-tokens with the same physical form have different meanings. An important 'borderline case' in this connection is that of sentences containing an implicit reference to time, such as 'Socrates is sitting down' (i.e. 'is sitting down now'). Aristotle, who discusses this example in the *Categories*, does not consider the possibility of using the phrase 'the same proposition' differently from the phrase 'the same sentence'; but he says that both the sentence or statements (λόγος) that someone is sitting, and the opinion (δόξα) that he it sitting, remain the same when uttered or entertained at different times; and accepts the consequence that the same statement, and the same opinion, may be true at one time and false at another (the statement or opinion that someone is sitting will be true so long as the person in question is in fact seated, and will become false—if it is persisted in—as soon as he rises). This manner of speaking, alike about 'sentences', 'statements' and 'propositions', persisted until quite recent times; but the common practice now is to use the term 'proposition' in such a way that its truth or falsehood cannot be said to alter with time. On this view, 'Socrates is sitting down' is not a genuine proposition but a movable part which may appear in a number of different propositions; and to make a complete proposition of it, we shall need to add some unambiguous indication of the precise time at which this particular down-sitting of Socrates is said to occur. 'Socrates is sitting down' is thought of, we might say, as a diary entry, with a date, hour, minute and second beside it, and this date, etc. is part of the 'proposition'. Of the complete proposition thus formed, we may say that if it is true at all it is true for ever, and similarly if it is false.

This modern usage also works the other way. It means not only that the one sentence 'Socrates is sitting down now' will be or express different propositions at different times, but also that the different sentences 'Socrates is sitting down now' and 'Socrates was sitting down then' will sometimes be or express the same proposition, as they may be referring *at* different times *to* the same time. Bosanquet,[1] in this connexion, introduced a distinction, which logicians of other schools than his have been glad to adopt,[2] between the 'time *of* predication' and the 'time *in* predication' (that is, between the time at which a proposition is uttered or a judgement made, and the time which the proposition or judgement is about). It is the time 'in' predication—the time that is part of its

---

[1] *Logic*, vol. 1, pp. 214 ff.

[2] See Keynes, *Formal Logic*, 4th ed., 50; P. Coffey, *The Science of Logic* (a Neo-Scholastic work in which extensive use is made of Keynes), vol. 1, pp. 161–2; Johnson, *Logic*, I.xiv.7.

'meaning'—that would now be generally taken as fixing the identity of a proposition, rather than the other, the time of its utterance (time 'of' predication), though this latter may affect the form of the sentence by which the proposition is expressed.[1]

CHAPTER TWO

The Aristotelian Account of Affirmation and Denial

The preliminary distinctions outlined at the beginning of the preceding chapter occupy the first four chapters of the *De Interpretatione*. In Chapter 5, the Proposition or Sentence Declaratory is divided into the simple, i.e. 'that which asserts or denies something of something', and the composite, i.e. 'that which is compounded of simple propositions'. (This 'composition' is, of course, of a higher order than that mentioned earlier as a feature of *every* kind of proposition.) In Chapter 6 we reach the topic which gives the whole work its unity—the conditions under which an affirmation and a denial may be regarded as giving mutually contradictory answers to the same question.

This chapter begins with two definitions, the extreme neatness of which rather disappears in the English, 'An affirmation is a positive assertion of something about something, a denial a negative assertion.'[1] (In the Greek, the difference between 'positive' and 'negative' is expressed simply by a pair of prepositions—affirmation, *kataphasis*, is *apophansis tinos kata tinos*, while negation, *apophasis*, is *apophansis tinos apo tinos*. This suggestive construction is reproduced in Boethius's Latin—*affirmatio* is *enunciatio alicuius de aliquo*, and *negatio*, *enunciatio alicuius ab aliquo*. It is as if we defined affirmation as saying a thing *of* something and negation as saying a thing *from* something.[2]) And what may be 'positively asserted' of anything (said 'of' it) Aristotle says in effect, may be 'negatively asserted' of that same thing (said 'from' it); so that 'every affirmation has an opposite denial, and similarly every denial an opposite affirmation'.[3]

---

[1] 17ᵃ25-6.

[2] In Apuleius the affirmative *enunciatio* is described as *dedicativa* ('of-speaking') and the negative as *abdicativa* ('from-speaking'). This, of course, corresponds quite exactly with *kataphasis* and *apophasis*.

[3] 17ᵃ31-2.

A *kataphasis* and *apophasis* which thus respectively affirm and deny the same predicate of the same subject constitute what Aristotle calls an *antiphasis* or 'contradictory pair'. Associated with the notion of such a 'contradictory pair' are two principles which are not explicitly stated here in the *De Interpretatione*, but which are presupposed throughout the book, and are explicitly mentioned in the *Posterior Analytics*[1] as assumed in our thinking on all subjects. (They are mentioned also in Aristotle's *Metaphysics*,[2] attempts to deny them being there subjected to detailed criticism.) These are the principle that 'it is impossible to affirm and deny simultaneously the same predicate of the same subject',[3] i.e. that the two members of an *antiphasis* cannot be true at once, and the principle that 'every predicate can be either truly affirmed or truly denied of every subject',[4] i.e. that at least one of the members of any *antiphasis* must be true. The former is generally called the 'Law of Contradiction' and the latter the 'Law of Excluded Middle' (because it excludes the possibility of a third case in which neither the *kataphasis* nor the *apophasis* is true), both being grouped with what is called the 'Law of Identity' —that anything may be truly affirmed of itself—under the general title of 'the laws of thought'. These laws also have other forms which we shall from time to time encounter.

The grouping of propositions into contradictory pairs is still one of the fundamental conceptions of logic. Thus Lord Russell says in *The Analysis of Mind*[5] that 'propositions occur in pairs, distinguished (in simple cases) by the absence or presence of the word "not"', and that the two members of such a pair have 'the same objective, but opposite meanings'—i.e. they refer to the same fact, but one points towards it and the other away from it—so that 'when one is true, the other is false, and when one is false, the other is true'. Aristotle does not mention 'objectives'; but he stresses the point that true contradictory opposition depends on the two statements being not only opposed in 'phase' (or 'quality', as the Latin logicians came to call it), i.e. on the one affirming and the other denying, but on their affirming and denying the same thing of the

---

[1] Book I, ch. II.
[2] Book I.
[3] *Anal. Post.* 77ª10–11.
[4] *Anal. Post.* 77ª22–3.
[5] p. 273.

same thing (*tou autou kata tou autou, eiusdem de eodem*), i.e. on their
having the same subject and predicate. He gives no examples,
but there is plainly no opposition between, say, 'Socrates is wise'
and 'Plato is not wise'—the second does not in this case contradict
the first, as 'Socrates is not wise' would do, but, literally, 'changes
the subject'. Similarly there is no opposition between 'Socrates is
wise' and 'Socrates is not unwell', where we change the predicate;
still less is there any between 'Socrates is wise' and 'Plato is not
unwell', where we change both. Moreover, this identity in the terms
of the affirmation and denial must be real; it is not enough to have
the same words, but used ambiguously (for 'Socrates is wise' and
'Socrates is not wise' to be genuinely opposed, we must be speaking
of the same Socrates in both statements, and must also mean the
same kind of 'wisdom'). And there are more complicated cautions
that must be given 'to meet the casuistries of sophists'; these form
the principal subject of the rest of the book. Aristotle, like Lord
Russell, is well aware that it is only 'in simple cases' that 'the
absence or presence of the word "not" ' is sufficient to mark off one
member of an *antiphasis* from the other.

The first complication, dealt with in Chapter 7, arises from the
fact that not all propositions concern 'individual' subjects (*singularia*)
like Socrates; some have 'universals', like 'man', for their subjects.
'By the term "universal",' Aristotle explains, 'I mean that which is
of such a nature as to be predicated of many subjects' (*quod de pluribus natum est praedicari*), 'by "individual" that which is not'.[1] This
possibility gives rise to a further distinction. A proposition which
has one of these 'universal' subjects may or may not be itself a
'universal proposition'. As examples of propositions which not only
have a universal subject but are themselves universal in character,
Aristotle gives 'Every man is white' and 'No man is white'. As
examples of propositions which have a universal subject but are not
'universal propositions', he first gives the bare 'Man is white' and
'Man is not white'. (The precise meaning attached by Aristotle to
this form of proposition is not very clear; it seems to have something
of the same ambiguity as sentences in English employing the indefinite article. When we say 'A man moves faster than a snail',
this means any and every man, and has the force of a 'universal'
proposition; but when we say 'A man is now running past the post"

[1] 17ᵃ38-9.

this is not about every man but only about some particular man.)
A little later Aristotle also mentions, as non-universal propositions
with universal subjects, the simple denials of universal ones—'Not
every man is white' (denying 'Every man is white') and 'Some man
is white' (denying 'No man is white'). Before touching on these,
though, he throws out what he considers a further illustration of the
fact that the word 'every' determines the character of the proposition
as a whole rather than of its subject. He points out what a curious
sort of proposition would result if we attached this word to the
subject and predicate of a proposition separately. 'Every man is an
animal' is a reasonable kind of proposition, and is in fact true; but
it is certainly not true that 'Every man is *every* animal', and Aristotle
surmises (incorrectly, we shall find) that no proposition of this form
is ever true.

A universal affirmation and a universal denial, he goes on, with
the same subject and the same predicate, are opposed to one another,
not as 'contradictories', but as 'contraries'. Each has its own contradictory; and while a pair of contrary propositions cannot be true
together, their respective contradictories can be. Thus while 'No
man is white' and 'Every man is white' are mutually inconsistent,
there is no such inconsistency between 'Some men are white' and
'Not every man is white'—these not only may be, but in fact are,
both true. But where we have a genuine pair of contradictories,
such as 'No man is white' and 'Some men are white', or 'Every man
is white' and 'Not every man is white', there must always be one
member of the pair true and the other false (so that to say 'No' to
one is to say 'Yes' to the other, and *vice versa*). This is the case also
with affirmations and denials with singular subjects, such as
'Socrates is white' and 'Socrates is not white'.

The term 'contrary' which Aristotle introduces here is often
employed by him, e.g. in the *Categories*, in a slightly different sense.
'Contraries' in this other sense are not propositions but attributes of
things, such as white and black, or good and bad. They are attributes of the same broad sort (both colours, like white and black, or
both moral qualities, like good and bad), and such that they cannot
both be present in the same subject in the same respect at the same
time; and they usually stand at opposite ends of a scale, the only
exception to this being the case in which there is no 'scale' because
no quality intermediate between the two contraries exists (as in the

case of odd and even). The sense of 'contrary' in which 'Every man is white' and 'No man is white' are called 'contrary propositions' seems to be derived from this different and more fundamental one. The parallelism between the two is plain enough. As contrary attributes are of the same general sort, so contrary propositions affirm and deny the same predicate of the same subject; as contrary attributes cannot inhere in the same subject at the same time, so contrary propositions cannot be true together; and as contrary attributes stand at opposite ends of a scale, in cases where intermediate attributes are possible, so contrary propositions stand at opposite ends of a scale, in cases where there are intermediate possibilities. Thus 'Every man is white' and 'No man is white' are opposite extremes, with the third possibility that some men are white and some not standing in between them. (The case in which there is no intermediate possibility might perhaps be illustrated by 'Socrates is white' and 'Socrates is not white', and here the notion of contrariety seems to merge into that of contradiction.)

In later chapters of the *De Interpretatione* other complications of the affirmation-denial pattern are discussed, such as those arising with ambiguous and composite propositions, and those arising with propositions which assert, not simply that something is or is not so, but that it may be or must be or cannot be so. We may note here some of the distinctions made in Chapter 10, which is a detailed discussion of affirmations and denials involving negative terms, i.e. the 'indefinite' nouns and verbs referred to in Chapters 2 and 3. The simplest form of proposition is said to be that which has some positive subject and the verb 'to be' for predicate, e.g. 'Man is' and 'Man is not'. Then we may have the forms 'Not-man is' and 'Not-man is not'; the 'universal' forms 'Every man is', 'Every man is not', 'Every not-man is', 'Every not-man is not'; and the past and future forms corresponding to all of these. More complicated are those forms in which 'is' is not the verb, but is a 'noun or verb' attached to the others as a third element (*triton proskatēgoreitai, tertium adjacens praedicatur*), as in 'Man is just'. Here the number of possible forms is doubled (since the addition of 'not' to 'is' and its addition to the predicate-term are no longer the same thing, and both are possible). Thus in place of the simple 'Man is' and 'Man is not' we have the four forms 'Man is just', 'Man is-not just', 'Man is not-just', 'Man is-not not-just', and the other forms that arise by replacing 'Man' by 'Not-man', or by 'Every man', or by 'Every not-man', or by 'Not every man', and so on. There are also propositions in which the verb 'is' does not appear at all, even as a *tertium adjacens*, the verb being some other one such as 'walks' or 'flourishes'.

Aristotle exhibits in this chapter a great fondness for arranging propositions in groups of four, but what he has to say on the relations between them is rather sketchy. He makes it clear that propositions with positive and negative subjects, such as 'Every man is just' and 'Whatever is not a man is just', are logically independent of one another; and as regards negative predicates, his position is more fully developed in a long chapter of the *Prior Analytics* (bk. I, ch. 46). His view is, briefly, that to say of any subject that it is not-white is not the same as to say that it is-not white, though it implies it, the four assertions 'It is white', 'It is-not white', 'It is not-white' and 'It is-not not-white' being related to one another in the same ways as 'Every man is just', 'Not every man is just', 'No man is just' and 'Some man is just'. 'It is white' and 'It is-not white' cannot be true or false of the same subject, just as 'Every man is just' and 'Not every man is just' cannot be true or false together; and there is the same relation between 'It is not-white' and 'It is-not not-white'. Being not-white implies not being white but is not implied by it, just as 'No man is just' implies 'Not every man is just' but is not implied by it; and being white and not being not-white are similarly related. 'It is white' and 'It is not-white' cannot be both true of the same subject, though they may both be false of it (i.e. it may be neither), just as 'Every man is just' and 'No man is just' cannot be both true, though they may be both false. These are the main points; and Aristotle has an interesting proof that if any four assertions A, B, C and D are related in certain of the ways indicated, they must be related in the other ways also. For suppose that one of the pair A and B must be true of any subject, but that of no subject can they both be true; suppose C and D to be similarly related; and suppose that if C is true of anything A must be, but not *vice versa*. Since wherever C is true A is, but A and B are never true of the subject, C and B will never be true of the same subject; and since either C or D must be true of any subject, wherever B is true (and C consequently not) D will be. There are other proofs of other details.

Aristotle's reasons for holding that a thing may be neither white nor not-white are some of them plainly bad and some of them obscure; but the Schoolmen interpreted this passage in the light of one in the *Categories* about 'contraries'. Here Aristotle draws a contrast between the opposition of the 'contrary' attributes 'well' and 'ill' and that of the contradictory propositions 'Socrates is ill' and 'Socrates is not ill', firstly on the obvious ground that one is an opposition of isolated terms and the other an opposition of entire propositions, but secondly on the ground that even if we expand 'well' and 'ill' to 'Socrates is ill' and 'Socrates is well', these propositions (though they cannot both be true at once) may both be false, whereas 'Socrates is ill' and 'Socrates is not ill' cannot be either true together or false together (one of them must be true). And his ground for saying that 'Socrates is ill' and 'Socrates is well' may both be false is not that the philosopher's health may be merely indifferent, but that he may not so much as exist, in which case of course he would be neither ill nor well. On the other hand, if we suppose Socrates to exist, he must obviously either be ill or not be ill, and the same is true even if he does not exist, for then he will not be ill. As regards the question raised in the *Prior Analytics*, the Schoolmen took Aristotle to mean that to be either white or not-white a thing must exist, whereas this is not necessary either for it not to be white or for it not to be not-white (if it doesn't exist, it isn't white, and isn't not-white either). They summed up his position in the maxims *ab est tertii ad est secundi adjecti valet consequentia affirmando* and *ab est secundi ad est tertii adjecti valet consequentia negando*. The first of these means that with affirmations we may validly infer, from a proposition in which 'is' functions as a *tertium adjacens* (such as 'Socrates is ill', or 'Socrates is not-white') the proposition with the same subject in which it functions as a predicate on its own ('Socrates is'); while with negations, we may validly infer, from a proposition in which 'is' functions as a predicate on its own (e.g. 'Socrates is not', i.e. does not exist) any other negation, with the same subject, in which 'is' functions as a *tertium adjacens* (e.g. 'Socrates is not ill', 'Socrates is not not-white').

One or two differences between the *Prior Analytics* and the *De Interpretatione*, where they touch upon the same subjects, may be noted. In the *De Interpretatione*, as we have seen, the proposition is called an *apophasis*, and thought of primarily as a member of a pair of contradictories, expressing the affirmative and negative to the same question. In the *Prior Analytics* it is generally called a *protasis* or premiss, marking the interest of this treatise in what can be inferred from a proposition rather than in how to express its opposite. One might illustrate the difference in point of view which the use of these two words suggests by reconsidering the relation between the propositions 'Socrates is wise', 'Plato is not wise', and 'Socrates is not unwell'. As was observed in the preceding section, though 'Socrates is wise' and 'Plato is not wise' respectively affirm and deny the same predicate of a subject, they do not affirm and deny it of the same subject, and so do not belong to the same 'pair of contradictories', and they may in fact be both true. When, however, we consider these two propositions as 'premisses', we see that, while not themselves opposed, their joint truth would nevertheless imply a certain opposition between their subject-terms; for from 'Socrates is wise' and 'Plato is not wise', we may infer, by what is called a syllogism in the second figure, that Plato is not Socrates, and that Socrates is not Plato. Again, we have observed that while 'Socrates is wise' and 'Socrates is not unwell' are respectively an affirmation and a denial concerning the same subject, they are not an affirmation and a denial of the same thing, so that there is no opposition between these two propositions either. But when we consider them as 'premisses', we see that their joint truth would imply, not quite an opposition, but at least a lack of connexion, between the 'wisdom' and the 'ill-health' which are affirmatively and negatively predicted in them; for from 'Socrates is wise' and 'Socrates is not unwell' we may infer, by what is called a syllogism in the third figure, that not everyone who is wise is unwell.

The *protasis* of the *Prior Analytics*, like the *apophansis* of the *De Interpretatione*, is 'a sentence affirming or denying one thing of another'.[1] It is 'either universal or particular or indefinite'. A 'universal' proposition or premiss states 'that something belongs to all or none of something else'; a 'particular', that it 'belongs to some or not to some or not to all' (the two negatives referred to here are the equivalent forms 'Some X is not Y' and 'Not all X is Y'); an 'indefinite', that it 'does or does not belong, without any mark to show whether it is universal or particular'.[2] The 'particulars' here

[1] *Prior Analytics* 24[a]16–17.
[2] *Prior Analytics* 24[a]19–20.

mentioned are the propositions which appear in the *De Interpretatione* as the simple contradictories, not themselves universal, of universal propositions; and the 'indefinites' are treated as having the same force for purposes of inference as the corresponding particulars. In Chapter 2 this classification is enlarged by a preliminary reference to the distinction between assertions of mere fact, of necessity, and of possibility. 'Every premiss states that something either is or must be or may be the attribute of something else; of premisses of these three kinds some are affirmative, others negative . . . ; again some affirmative and negative premisses are universal others particular, others indefinite.'

In neither of these classifications is any use made of the distinction drawn in the *De Interpretatione* between propositions with 'universal' subjects and those with 'individual' subjects, and in fact propositions with individual subjects—'singular' propositions, as logicians came later to call them—are very little discussed in this treatise. The *Prior Analytics* differs from the *De Interpretatione*, again, in the way in which propositions are analysed into their parts. The basic units are no longer the Platonic 'noun' and 'verb', but rather a pair of 'terms' united by 'is' or 'is not'.[1] That is, of the three broad types of proposition illustrated in the *De Interpretatione* by 'Man is', 'Man is just', 'Man walks', the only one used here is the second; though more frequently Aristotle uses a more oblique form in which the predicate is put first and said to 'belong' (*huparchein*) to the subject. Thus 'Every B is A' appears as 'The A belongs to all the B' (so literally: the most accurate rendering of the meaning might be 'A-ness attaches to the entire class of B's'). This manner of speaking makes possible a high degree of abstraction, and Aristotle is able to speak of the relations 'belonging to all', 'not belonging to all', 'belonging to some' and 'not belonging to any' as if they were *terms* predicable of various subject-predicate pairs just as 'being white', 'not being white', 'being not-white' and 'not being not-white' are predicable of various objects.

[1] *Anal. Pr.* 24^{b}16–18.

CHAPTER THREE

The Kinds of Terms

1. *Subjects and predicates*

The immediate constituents of categorical propositions are terms. Of terms, we have hitherto spoken only incidentally; we must now focus our attention more directly upon them. We shall begin with the traditional account.

'I call that a term (*horos*),' Aristotle says in the *Prior Analytics*,[1] 'into which the proposition (*protasis*) is resolved, that is, both the predicate and that of which it is predicated, "being" or "not being" being added.' Turning to the classical English logicians, we read in Watts[2] 'A *Proposition* is a Sentence wherein two *Ideas* or *Terms* are joined or disjoined by one Affirmation or Negation'; there are, therefore, 'three Things which go to the Nature and Constitution of a Proposition, (viz.) the *Subject*, the *Predicate* and the *Copula*. The *Subject* of a Proposition is that concerning which any thing is affirmed or denied . . . The *Predicate* is that which is affirmed or denied of the Subject . . . The *Subject* and *Predicate* of a Proposition taken together are called the *Matter* of it; for these are the Materials of which it is made. The *Copula* is the *Form* of a Proposition; it represents the Act of the Mind affirming or denying.' Whately tells much the same story. 'A Syllogism,' he says,[3] 'being . . . resolvable into three Propositions, and each Proposition containing two Terms; of these Terms, that which is spoken of is called the *subject*; that which is said of it, the *predicate*.' Between these terms, and distinct from them, is placed 'the Copula, which indicates the act of Judgment, as by it the Predicate is affirmed or denied of the Subject'. Finite verbs, Whately insists, are not in this sense 'terms', though they contain terms; and the predicate term of a proposition is only identifiable when its verb has been turned into 'is' or 'is not' plus

---

[1] 24^{b}16–18.
[2] *Logick*, II.i.
[3] *Elements*, II.i.2.

49

something which is not a verb. 'The substantive-verb' (i.e. 'to be'), he goes so far as to say, 'is the only *verb* recognised by Logic; inasmuch as all others are compound; being resolvable, by means of the verb "to be", and a participle or adjective: e.g. "the Romans conquered": the word conquered is both copula and predicate, being equivalent to "*were* (Cop.) *victorious* (Pred.)".'

J. S. Mill[1] repeats the substance of this traditional account, but varies its details. He nowhere defines 'term', and for the most part (like Hobbes before him) he speaks not of terms but of 'names'. He analyses propositions in the usual manner. 'Every proposition consists of three parts: the Subject, the Predicate and the Copula. The predicate is the name denoting that which is affirmed or denied. The subject is the name denoting the person or thing which something is affirmed or denied of. The copula is the sign denoting that there is an affirmation or denial.' These definitions differ from those quoted in the preceding paragraph in one important particular. In Mill, it is clear that subject, predicate and copula are all of them *words*, the first two being 'names' and the last a 'sign'. In the others, this is by no means so clear, especially in the case of 'subject'. In Mill, the subject of a proposition is the 'name denoting' what that proposition is about; but in Watts and Whately (and also in Aristotle) the subject of a proposition is itself what that proposition is about (it is 'that concerning which any thing is affirmed or denied', 'that which is spoken of'). The subject, in this latter sense, will not in general be a word; for though we do sometimes make statements about words, most of our statements are about other things. Thus 'Socrates is wise' is not about the word 'Socrates'—it is not the word that is said to be wise—but about Socrates the man. Socrates the man, therefore, rather than 'Socrates' the word, is the subject of this proposition, if the definitions of Watts and Whately are to be accepted, and taken at their face value. But the subject of a proposition is one of the 'terms' of that proposition; and could Socrates the man be seriously described as a 'term'? Whatever may be the case with 'subject', must not a 'term' be a word? Mill by-passes this question by speaking of 'names' rather than 'terms', and by defining a proposition's 'subject' quite explicitly as a word. As to earlier logicians, their use of 'term' fluctuates—sometimes they do speak of a non-verbal object, such as the man Socrates, as a term; sometimes

[1] *System of Logic*, I.i.2.

only of what signifies this object. In many contexts this confusion is in fact unimportant; where it is not unimportant, Joseph[1] suggests that we should distinguish between the 'term of thought' (in the case of the subject-term, that which is thought or spoken about) and the 'term verbal' (that in the proposition by which the term of thought is signified).

The distinction between the 'matter' and the 'form' of a proposition, which we have encountered in the passage from Watts, seems to reflect the ascriptive or multiple-relation theory of believing. The subject and the predicate—the proposition's 'matter'—seem to be or indicate what is being ascribed to (or denied of) what, while the copula indicates the mental act of ascribing (or denying). But is the copula really the only element of form, even in this sense of 'form', in a categorical proposition? What about the sign of quantity, if the proposition has one? The voice of tradition is a little uncertain at this point. On the one hand, when the medieval logicians distinguished between 'formal' and 'material' consequences, they had no hesitation at all in including the quantity of the propositions involved among the elements which may go to the making of a 'true formal consequence'. On the other hand, one finds a tendency among the older writers to treat the sign of quantity as part of the subject-term. Thus Watts says that 'propositions may be divided according to their *Subject* into *universal* and *particular*'; and he goes on to speak of '*universal, indefinite* and *particular* Terms', meaning by this such expressions as 'Every man', 'Man' *simpliciter*, and 'Some man'.[1]

This way of talking has most to be said for it in the case of singular subjects formed by attaching an 'individualising prefix' to a common noun, as in 'This Hottentot' or 'The present King of England'. It is easy to think of these as complex proper names, and proper names are certainly terms. The older writers also found it easy to extend the treatment of 'This' or 'The' as parts of a term to 'A' or 'A certain', and so to 'Some'; and if to 'Some', why not to 'Every'? But, as at least some of the older logicians were aware, the treatment of 'Some X' and 'Every X' as terms raises serious formal difficulties. One mentioned by Peter of Spain[3] is this: When the middle term of a syllogism is complex (or as he puts it, when it is qualified in some

---

[1] *Introduction to Logic*, 2nd ed., p. 21.
[2] *Logick*, II.ii.1.
[3] *Summulae* (Bochenski's edition), 12.07–08.

way), the entire term (or the term with its qualification) must appear at both points for the syllogistic conclusion to be drawn. Thus with the major premiss 'Every white man is running', we can only draw the conclusion 'Socrates is running' if our minor is 'Socrates is a white man'—'Socrates is a man' will not do. But 'Socrates is a white man' is sufficient—we do not need to make it 'Socrates is *every* white man', as we would have to do if 'every' were really a further qualification of the subject (or in modern parlance part of it) like 'white'. Peter's solution is that while 'every' does signify a qualification of the subject, it does not signify a qualification of 'that which is the subject' (*id quod est subiectum*) but rather of the subject *as* subject (*subiectum in quantum subiectum*), i.e. of its subjecthood. In other words, it does not tell us anything further about what it is that 'falls under' the predicate, but rather tells us in what way this 'falling under' occurs.

The transition to a more straightforward solution of this problem may be traced in the successive editions of Keynes's *Formal Logic*. In the first edition[1] Keynes takes over the common account of the matter without criticism, and says that 'in logical analysis, the categorical proposition always consists of three parts, namely, two terms which are united by a copula'. By way of illustration, he turns 'All that love virtue love angling' into 'All lovers of virtue are lovers of angling', and gives 'All lovers of virtue' as the subject, 'is' as the copula and 'lovers of angling' as the predicate. Elsewhere, all the same, in the same edition,[2] he describes 'All S is P' as 'a proposition having S for its subject', not as one having 'All S'; and this inconsistency is not uncommon where logicians use symbols.[3] In the appropriate section of his second edition,[4] Keynes repeats his first story, and again gives 'All lovers of virtue' as a subject-term; but he adds at the end that 'to complete our analysis we ought to note a fourth element in the categorical proposition, namely the sign of quantity attached to the subject'. He also adds a footnote to the next section, to the effect that 'the subject and predicate of a proposition constitute its *matter*, while its quantity and quality constitute its *form*'—its quantity, note, and not its quality only. In

[1] §36.
[2] §66.
[3] Cf. Joseph, *Introduction to Logic*, 2nd ed., p. 170.
[4] §35.

the third edition, the inconsistency is removed, the relevant section[1] opening with the statement that 'a categorical proposition consists of two names (which are respectively the *subject* and the *predicate*), united by a *copula*, and usually preceded by a sign of quantity', so that it 'contains four elements, two of which—the subject and the predicate—constitute its matter, while the remaining two—the copula and the sign of quantity—constitute its form'. This is repeated in the fourth edition[2] with no alteration except the substitution of 'two terms' for 'two names'; and in both of the later editions the subject of 'All lovers of virtue love angling' is given as 'lovers of virtue', without the 'All'.

One way of reconciling the admission that the sign of quantity is an element of form in a proposition with the old description of the form of a proposition as its copula, is of course to treat the sign of quantity as part of the copula. The position of Petrus Hispanus is not far from this; and in the modern period, Mrs Ladd-Franklin specifically treated the eight propositional forms of de Morgan as having so many different copulas—'Every . . . is . . .'; 'Not every . . . is . . .'; 'No . . . is . . .'; 'Some . . . is . . .'; 'Only . . . is . . .'; 'Not only . . . is . . .'; 'There is nothing besides . . . and . . .'; and 'There is something besides . . . and . . .'—and for each of them she has a special symbol.[3] There is a suggestion of this solution in a simple symbolic device which Keynes takes over from Ueberweg even in his first edition—the representation of 'Every S is P' as 'S a P', of 'No S is P' as 'S e P', of 'Some S is P' as 'S i P', and of 'Some S is not P' as 'S o P'. A crude adumbration of this device was employed by an earlier writer than Ueberweg, namely Drobitsch, who, in dealing with syllogisms, used such names as '*mapsamsap*' (for Barbara), '*pemsamsep*' (for Cesare), etc. The modern Polish use of such symbols as 'Aab' (or 'Uab') for universal affirmatives, 'Eab' (or 'Yab') for universal negatives, 'Iab' for particular affirmatives, and 'Oab' for particular negatives, modifies the symbolism of Ueberweg and Keynes in the same way as Łukasiewicz's symbolism for hypotheticals modifies that of *Principia Mathematica*.

In contrast to this multiplication of copulae, it has sometimes been contended that there is only one copula, the sign of affirmation,

[1] §39.
[2] §62.
[3] *Baldwin's Dictionary of Philosophy & Psychology*, vol. 2, p. 369.

and that what is called denying a predicate of a subject is really just affirming the corresponding negative term. Hobbes, in particular, both makes signs of quantity parts of the subject-term and makes the sign of negation part of the predicate-term. If we attempt to assign a meaning, not itself involving the notion of denial, to the term allegedly thus predicated, we shall find that any such meaning involves a secondary quantification—'Bucephalus is a not-man' must mean either 'Bucephalus is other than *every*thing that is human', or '*Every* attribute of Bucephalus is other than the attribute of humanity', or 'Bucephalus has *some* attribute that is incompatible with humanity' (or 'Bucephalus is something-incompatible-with-being-human'), incompatibility or repugnancy being regarded as a certain indefinable relation which holds between certain characters.[1] Thus, instead of making the sign of quantity modify the copula like a sign of negation, this view defines the sign of negation in terms of a sign of quantity, together with some indefinable relative term (either 'other than' or 'incompatible with'). This possibility has been considered especially in connection with attempts to eliminate 'negative facts' from the furniture of the universe, i.e. to avoid the view that the kind of fact which makes a denial true is irreducibly different in its structure from the kind of fact which verifies an affirmation.[2]

The main current symbolisms in effect have only an affirmative copula, but instead of defining 'not' in terms of a sign of quantity, assimilate it to the connectives 'if', 'and', etc. which appear in the logic of hypotheticals. For the one (affirmative) copula there is no separate symbol; in such a propositional form as 'fa', that it is F is said of A simply by the juxtaposition of the two symbols. In the form 'Nfa' the function of the symbol 'N' is a little ambiguous. We may regard it as modifying the 'f', so that what is said of A by this form is that it is not-F; or we may regard it as modifying the whole proposition 'fa', so that what is being said here is that it is not the

---

[1] The first two of alternatives are suggested in G. F. Stout's *Studies in Philosophy and Psychology*, p. 346. For the 'incompatibility' view, see Johnson's 'Analysis of thinking', *Mind* 1918, pp. 148–51.

[2] See R. Demos, 'A Discussion of a Certain Type of Negative Proposition', *Mind* 1917 (against 'negative facts') and B. Russell, *On Propositions: What They Are and How They Mean*, Arist. Soc. Supp. Vol. II (1919), pp. 3–6 (in their favour). For other deliverances on this and allied points, see Joseph's *Introduction*, 2nd ed., pp. 171–4; Keynes's *Formal Logic*, 4th ed., §85; and Johnson's *Logic*, i.v.1–2.

case that A is F. But in any case it is plain that the attachment of 'N' to the expression 'fa' is not an alternative to the juxtaposition of 'f' and 'a' but presupposes it, and also that 'N' comes out of the same box as such symbols as 'C', 'A' and 'K'. (Of 'Cfaga', which might mean 'If Caesar is a tyrant he deserves death', we can similarly ask whether it is being here said of A that if it is F it is G—of Caesar, that he is deserving-of-death-if-a-tyrant—or whether it is being said that if it is the case that A is F then it is the case that A is G.)[1]

However it is interpreted, and whereuntosoever it may be attached, the sign of negation, like the signs of quantity, is unhesitatingly placed by all logicians among the elements which may go to the making of a 'true formal consequence'.

2. *Categoremata and syncategoremata*

We have used the term 'term' so far in an essentially relative sense. We have written as if a term were always a term *of* some proposition (its subject or its predicate). But derived from this relative sense is an 'absolute' one. For we may not only speak of some word or more complex expression T as the subject- or predicate-term of some given proposition P, but may also speak of it simply as a 'term', in itself. An expression is a 'term' in this sense if it is capable of functioning as a 'term' in the other sense, i.e. as the subject or predicate of a proposition, even though it may not be a term of the particular proposition in which we are considering it, if indeed we are considering it in a proposition at all. Thus we may say that 'virtue', in 'All lovers of virtue love angling', is a 'term' in this derivative sense, though it is not a term of this proposition but merely a part of one (part of the subject-term 'lovers of virtue');

[1] Even of such a proposition as 'If Caesar is a saint then Brutus deserves death', which might be symbolised as 'Cfagb'—we might ask whether it is being said of Brutus that he is deserving-of-death-if-Caesar-is-a-saint, or of Caesar that he is a-saint-only-if-Brutus-is-deserving-of-death, or of Caesar and Brutus that if the former is a saint then the latter deserves death; or just that if (it is the case that) Caesar is a saint then (it is the case that) Brutus deserves death. The existence of three alternative 'predicative' interpretations may be parallelled with 'N' when we consider such a proposition as 'Richard does not love Joan', symbolised as 'Nfab'. Here, besides regarding the 'N' as modifying the whole proposition 'fab', we may regard it as modifying 'f*b', so that the whole says of Richard that he is not-a-lover-of-Joan, or 'fa', so that the whole says of Joan that she is not-loved-by-Richard, or just 'f', so that the whole says of Richard and Joan that the former does not love the latter.

for it may easily be used as a complete term in some other proposition, such as 'Virtue is its own reward'. It has always, so to speak, the 'potentiality' of functioning as a term, even if in a given proposition this potentiality is not actualised.

Expressions which thus have the capacity for functioning as terms, whether or not they are actually being so used, were called by the later medieval logicians 'categorematic' expressions. The opposite of 'categorematic' is 'syncategorematic'. Sometimes categorematic expressions are called 'significative', and syncategorematic ones 'consignificative'. Both 'consignificative' and still more 'syncategorematic' suggest that although the expressions in question are not capable of standing alone as terms of a proposition, they may do so in combination with other words. This would seem to exclude the copula, and also (if we regard them as outside the subject) signs of quantity, from both classes;[1] but such words may enter into subject or predicate terms which are complex enough to contain secondary quantifications (e.g. the predicate of 'Some Frenchmen are haters of all Germans', which contains 'all') or subordinate clauses (e.g. the subject of 'No fisherman who is a lover of virtue will take advantage of a short supply to raise the price of his goods', which subject contains 'is'). The same consideration—that they may be parts of terms which contain subordinate clauses—perhaps also takes care of finite verbs, which are neither terms nor (usually) parts of terms, but contain terms as their own parts. Minto[2] suggests 'hypercategorematic' for these; an older description of them is 'mixed'.[3] 'Mixed term', it should be noted, is a solecism, and so is 'syncategorematic term', since the former is more than a term and the latter less; though Mill uses both expressions.[4]

---

[1] Cf. C. S. Peirce (*Collected Papers*, 2.331): 'The Copula seems to fall between two stools, being neither categorematic nor syncategorematic.'

[2] *Logic, Inductive and Deductive*, p. 69.

[3] So, e.g. Whately, *Elements*, II.i.3: 'A verb (all except the substantive verb used as a copula) is a *mixed* word, being resolvable into the Copula and Predicate to which it is equivalent.'

[4] *System of Logic*, I.ii.2. Mill rules that a 'mixed term' is really categorematic; but he completely misunderstands the usual sense of 'mixed'. A mixed term, he says, is 'a combination of one or more Categorematic, and one or more Syncategorematic words, as A heavy body, or A court of justice'. Such a combination, as he rightly enough observes, is no more than a 'many-worded name', and is 'in the only useful sense of the word, Categorematic'; but it is not, in the proper sense, 'mixed'.

The clearest instances of syncategorematic words are perhaps prepositions; and of categorematic words, nouns.[1] Adjectives are more of a problem, and whether or not they are categorematic used to be often disputed. Some words which are generally classified by grammarians as adjectives are certainly not categorematic, namely the signs of quantity 'Some' and 'Every'—we cannot say 'Every is so-and-so' or 'So-and-so is every'. But precisely this fact is a ground for questioning whether such words are usefully classified as adjectives at all; they seem to belong rather with the articles 'A' and 'The'.[2] Confining ourselves to 'descriptive' adjectives, it would seem on the face of it that they may function on their own as predicate-terms, but only as parts of subject-terms. We say 'Socrates is wise', but not 'A wise is so-and-so', only 'A wise man is so-and-so' ('A wise man keeps his own counsel'), or the like. But that is perhaps a linguistic accident; in Latin and Greek, as Mill reminds us,[3] adjectives may be subjects too. He gives 'White is a colour' as a parallel case in English; but this is not quite accurate, for 'white' here means 'whiteness', and is not an adjective but an abstract noun. A better parallel might be 'The dead ought not to be maligned', or 'The brave deserve a monopoly of the fair'. It would usually be said that in such sentences the true subject is some noun that is 'understood'—what is meant is 'Dead *people* ought not to be maligned', and 'Brave *men* deserve, etc.'. The adjective here is an abbreviation or 'grammatical ellipsis' for an adjectivally qualified noun. And this is precisely what is said, by those who deny that adjectives are categorematic, of all apparent uses of adjectives as entire terms. 'Socrates is wise', it is argued, means 'Socrates is a wise man', or at all events a 'wise being'. For an adjective is never, in its meaning, complete in itself—there is always an implied reference to something qualified. In medieval terminology, it is not an 'absolute term' but a 'connotative term' (though the use of the word 'term' in this context implies the classification of adjectives as categorematic all the same). This implicit reference to something else is indicated by the very name 'adjective'—it is a word that is

---

[1] At least in the nominative case. Of nouns in oblique cases, we shall have something to say in Chapter 4.

[2] They are thus classified, e.g., in Joseph's *Introduction* (2nd ed.) p. 19, n. 1, and in Johnson's *Logic*, I.vii.1. Johnson calls them 'applicatives'.

[3] *System of Logic*, I.ii.2.

designed to be attached to another. Consistently with this position, it is sometimes held that a sentence is not in 'logical form' until its predicate-term is expressed as a noun (with or without a qualifying adjective). And in support of this it may be pointed out that when a categorical proposition is converted, an adjectivally-expressed predicate must be turned into a noun, or have a noun supplied, in order to form the subject of the converse (as when we convert 'Some men are wise' to 'Some wise beings are men'); so that the predicate-term must 'really' have been a noun all the time.

We shall leave this question at this point for the present, though we shall later see that there are good reasons for reversing the opinion just set out. But before leaving this distinction between categorematic and syncategorematic words, we may note that it was customary among the older logicians to point out, in connection with this distinction, that there is one way in which not only descriptive adjectives but even prepositions, articles and signs of quantity may stand alone as subject-terms of propositions. 'Every', for example, does appear to function as a subject when we use it in such a sentence as '*Every* is a sign of quantity' (similarly with 'Of' in '*Of* is a preposition'). The Latin logicians described the subject of such a sentence as having 'material supposition' (*suppositio materialis*), meaning by this that it here stands for itself as a word; and they admitted that any word at all could function as a term if used in this 'non-significative' way. They therefore defined a syncategorematic word as one which could not stand by itself as a subject or predicate if used significatively, i.e. with ordinary and not 'material' supposition.[1] Most logicians of the present day, however, would say that 'Every', in '*Every* is a sign of quantity', is a totally different word from 'Every' in, say, 'Every lover of virtue is a lover of angling'. 'Every' (without italics) is a sign of quantity,

---

[1] See Moody's *Logic of William of Ockham*, p. 42 and n. The medieval qualification is also made by Mill (op. cit.), though it does not appear in the discussion of categorematic and syncategorematic words in Whately's *Elements* (I.i.3). This is one of the points at which Mill's development of Whately consists in fuller utilisation of the logical distinctions made by the later Schoolmen; and I suspect that his use of this one here is largely responsible for its preservation by some relatively modern writers who do not mention *suppositio materialis* at any other point—e.g. Keynes, *Studies and Exercises*, 1st ed., §2; 2nd and 3rd eds., §5; Joseph, *Introduction to Logic* (2nd ed.), p. 19; and even the Neo-Scholastic P. Coffey (*The Science of Logic*, vol. 1, p. 37).

and as such is incapable of standing alone as the subject or predicate of any proposition whatever; while '*Every*' (italicised) is not a sign of quantity, but a proper name—a name, in fact, of the (unitalicised) word 'Every'.[1] This does not mean that the statement '*Every* is a sign of quantity' is false; for this statement does not assert that '*Every*' (italicised) is a sign of quantity, but rather that that of which '*Every*' is a name, i.e. the unitalicised 'Every', is a sign of quantity (just as 'Socrates is wise' does not attribute wisdom to the name 'Socrates', but to him whose name it is), and this is true. This is, in fact, just a special case of the distinction between the 'term of thought' and the 'term verbal', made a little tricky by the fact that the term of thought here happens to be itself a word.

3. *Types of ambiguity*

In none of Aristotle's logical writings do we find any chapter in which he sets out to classify terms in as many different ways as possible; though such chapters (or sections) are a customary feature of the later common logics.[2] Most of the distinctions made by the later writers are, however, to be found in various parts of the *Organon*, and especially in the *Categories*; and we shall consider them as they appear there, indicating as we go along what the later writers have made of them.

The *Categories* opens with the assertion that 'Things are said to be named "equivocally" when, though they have a common name, the definition corresponding with the name differs for each', but 'are said to be named "univocally" ' when they 'have both the name and the definition answering to the name in common'.[3] We should note here the carefulness of Aristotle's wording. The word 'Animal' is not ambiguous because it is applied both to men and to oxen, for it conveys the same fact about both, or as Aristotle puts it, we would give the same definition for the word in both its applications; but where words are genuinely equivocal, this is not the case. Closer attention to this point might have obviated some mistakes in later

---

[1] For this point of view see, e.g., W. V. Quine's *Mathematical Logic*, §4; and A. Tarski, *Introduction to Logic*, §18.

[2] See, e.g., Watts's *Logick*, i.iv; Whately's *Elements*, ii.v.i; Mill's *System*, i.ii; Jevons's *Elementary Lessons*, iii; Keynes's *Studies and Exercises* (4th ed.), i.i; Joseph's *Introduction*, ch. 2.

[3] *Cat.* 1ª1–2, 7–8.

writers. Watts, for example, argues that 'Words alter their Significations according to the *Ideas of the various Persons, Sects* or *Parties* who use them', and to illustrate this, asserts that 'when a *Jew* speaks of the *true Religion*, he means the *Institution of Moses*; when a *Turk* mentions it, he intends the *Doctrine of Mahomet*', and so on.[1] Whately corrects Watts here, classifying this as a 'real' question or matter of dispute which is mistakenly treated as merely verbal. 'Ambiguity,' he says, may be 'erroneously attributed to some term, when different persons who in reality employ it in the *same sense*, are accustomed to *apply* it differently'; 'the term "true-believer" ', for example 'which is applied by Mahometans to a believer in the Koran, would be considered by Christians as more applicable to a believer in the Gospel; but it would not be correct to say that "the one party *means* by this term, so and so, and the other, something different": for they do not attach *different senses to the word* "true", or to the word "believe"; they differ only in their persuasions of what *is* true, and *ought* to be believed.'[2] This distinction between 'sense' and 'application' is one which we shall encounter again.

Beside 'things which are named equivocally' and 'things which are named univocally', Aristotle mentions, in this first chapter of the *Categories*, things which are named 'derivatively', such as 'grammar' and 'grammarian'. In later writers, this supplement to the article *De Aequivocis* is often replaced by one on the use of words 'analogically'. Though not touched upon just at this point, this is a thoroughly Aristotelian topic. In a well-known passage in the *Metaphysics*,[3] for example, Aristotle refers to the different but analogical uses of the word 'healthy'. He has in mind its uses in such phrases as 'healthy food', 'a healthy complexion', a 'healthy body'. It is no mere accident that the same word is used in these different cases, since all its uses are 'related to one central point'. 'Everything which is healthy is related to health, one thing in the sense that it preserves health, another in the sense that it produces it, another in the sense that it is a symptom of health, another because it is capable of it.' And in the same way there are different but not unconnected senses of 'being', as when a thing or 'substance' is said to exist, and its weight is said to exist also. The reference to

[1] *Logick*, I.iv.8.
[2] *Elements*, IV.iv.2.
[3] 1003^{a}32–^{b}10.

'substances' (things), according to Aristotle, is always present—'some things are said to be because they are substances, others because they are affections of substance', and so on. In some writers analogy is treated as merely a particular case of ambiguity; and no doubt it is that, but it perhaps has sufficient importance to merit separate consideration. The various uses of the term 'term' itself are for the most part analogical. Thus when the word 'Socrates' and the man Socrates are both said to be the subject-term of the proposition 'Socrates is wise', we have not a mere accidental equivocation, but the subject-term in the one sense is the word used to name the subject-term in the second sense; and when a word in isolation is said to be a term, it is because, even though it is not actually doing so, it is capable of functioning as a 'term of a proposition'.

It is questionable whether 'term' is really the substantive to which the adjective 'ambiguous' (or 'equivocal') ought properly to be attached. Mill argued that 'an aequivocal or ambiguous word is not one name, but two names, accidentally coinciding in sound', and that '*file* meaning a steel instrument, and *file* meaning a line of soldiers, have no more title to be considered one word, because written alike, than *grease* and *Greece* have, because they are pronounced alike'. They are, he says, 'one sound'; that is all.[1] And all other logicians agree with him when it comes to the practical point of deciding what words may be substituted for two different occurrences of the same letter in a propositional or inferential form (e.g. for the two Ys in 'Every X is Y and every Y is Z').

4. *Abstract and concrete, singular and general*
'Of things themselves', Aristotle says, towards the beginning of ch. 2 of the *Categories*, 'some are predicable of a subject, and are never present in a subject . . . Some things, again, are present in a subject, but are never predicable of a subject . . . Other things, again, are both predicable of a subject and present in a subject . . . There is, lastly, a class of things which are neither present in a subject nor predicable of a subject.' We might perhaps re-phrase this as follows: What a term means, may be (1) something that a given subject may *be*, but cannot *have*, e.g. a man. Socrates may 'be a man' (in Aristotle's terminology, 'man' is 'predicable of' such a subject), but he cannot 'have a man', in the sense in which he

[1] *System of Logic*, I.ii.8.

may have wisdom, or manhood (in Aristotle's terminology, 'man' is not 'present in' a subject). Or a term may mean (2) something that a subject may have, but cannot be. Aristotle's examples are some particular point of knowledge that a mind may have ('the knowledge of this', say), though the mind 'is' not that point of knowledge; and some particular shade of whiteness that a body may have, though the body would not be said to 'be' this whiteness. Or a term may mean (3) something that some subjects may have and others may be; e.g. knowledge, which the mind may have, and which grammatical-knowledge, for example, is. Or a term may mean (4) something that no subject either has or is, e.g. an individual man or horse ('this man', 'this horse'). No doubt Pegasus may be said to 'be' Pegasus, and for that matter the knowledge that *mensa* is feminine may be said to 'be' the knowledge that *mensa* is feminine, but not in quite the same sense of 'be' as that in which Pegasus 'is' a horse. (This distinction will become clearer later.)

Modern logicians would query Aristotle's apparent assumption that there are four different kinds of 'things' in question here; but he has at least drawn attention to two important distinctions among 'terms verbal', namely the distinctions which appear in Mill as those (a) between 'individual names' (such as 'Pegasus') and 'general names' (such as 'man') and (b) between 'abstract names' (such as 'whiteness') and 'concrete names' (such as, again, 'Pegasus' or 'man'). Mill's 'general names' are those which Aristotle would describe as naming things that are 'predicable of' a subject, and his 'abstract names' are those which Aristotle would describe as naming things that may be 'present in' a subject. And like Aristotle, Mill makes these two distinctions cut cross one another, giving four divisions in all. He insists in particular that not only concrete but also abstract names may be general as well as singular. 'A concrete name is a name which stands for a thing; an abstract name is a name which stands for an attribute of a thing'; and of abstract names, 'some . . . are certainly general', namely 'those which are names not of one single or definite attribute, but of a class of attributes. Such is the word *colour*, which is a name common to whiteness, redness, etc. Such is even the word whiteness, in respect of the different shades of whiteness to which it is applied in common; the word magnitude, in respect of the various degrees of magnitude and various dimensions of space.' But an abstract name is singular 'when only one attribute, neither variable in degree nor in kind, is designated by the name; as visibleness; tangibleness; equality; squareness; milkwhiteness'.[1]

Connected with Mill's distinction between classes of attributes and individual attributes falling under them, is the distinction drawn in the present century by Johnson[2] between what he calls 'determinate' and 'determinable' characters. A specific shade of whiteness and a specific shade of redness would by Mill's account belong to different classes of attributes—one to the class of 'shades of whiteness' and one to the class of 'shades of redness'. A specific shade of whiteness and, let us say, a specific shape (such as equilateral triangularity) would also belong to different classes of attributes; but they plainly do so in a much more radical sense than the former pair. The specific shade of whiteness and the specific shade of redness are both of them colours; but the specific shape (though it too is an 'attribute') is something quite different. The colour and the shape, Johnson would say, fall under different 'determinables'. A determinable or determinable character is what we are indicating by the word 'respect' when we say that a pair of objects resemble one another in one respect and differ from one another in some other respect. It is, as Johnson says, what the older logical writers meant by a *fundamentum divisionis* or basis of division. Thus one thing might resemble another in respect of its shape, but might differ from it in respect of its colour, and we may divide things according to their shapes or their colours; colour and shape are typical Johnsonian determinables. Specific shapes and colours are called by Johnson 'determinates' under these determinables. There seems to be some sort of incompatibility or repugnancy between the different determinates under the same determinable, so that no object can be characterised by more than one of them at once (though this often has to be said with qualifications—in the case of colours, not more than one at the same point; and in the case of pitches of sound, it is not easy to say just what is the qualification required). The 'contraries' discussed in Aristotle's *Categories* seem to be different determinates under the same determinable; and those logicians, especially since Kant, who have preferred to use 'either' in the exclusive sense seem to have had in mind especially

[1] *System of Logic*, I.ii.4.
[2] *Logic*, Part I, ch. 11.

disjunctions like 'Whatever has shape is either triangular or square or circular, etc.' The repugnancy between determinates under the same determinable seems also to be what those writers chiefly have in mind who attempt to define negation in terms of 'incompatibility'. We often (as with colours) have no words for completely determinate characters, nor any power of distinguishing them; but we generally assume that the characters of things are in fact absolutely determinate, and we often have groups of words (such as 'reddish', 'red', 'scarlet') which approach more and more closely to the ascription of such completely determinate characters to things. Some modern writers[1] have made Mill's point about these words by saying that statements in which they are used implicitly contain a secondary quantification—'This is red' means 'This is of *some* shade of redness'; 'This is not red', 'This is of *no* shade of redness'.

The distinction between individual and general names, or rather between individual and general 'things', reappears in Aristotle's *De Interpretatione* as the distinction between individual and 'universal' subjects of propositions; and that between abstract and concrete names reappears in a different form later in the *Categories*. Dealing with the category of Quality, Aristotle notes that associated with the name of a quality is usually another word, an adjective, which is applied to 'that which is qualified'. 'Thus the terms "whiteness", "grammar", "justice", give us the adjectives "white", "grammatical", "just" and so on.'[2] It is, in fact, this passage rather than the other which is most plainly echoed in what later writers have to say on the distinction between abstract and concrete. '*Abstract* Terms,' says Watts,[3] 'signify the Mode or Quality of a Being, without Regard to the Subject in which it is; as *Whiteness, Roundness, Length, Breadth, Wisdom, Mortality, Life, Death. Concrete* Terms, while they express the Quality, do also either express, or imply, or refer to some Subject to which it belongs; as *white, round, long, broad, wise, mortal, living, dead.*' Watts adds, however, that concrete terms 'are not always *Noun Adjectives* in a grammatical Sense; for a *Fool*, a *Knave*, a *Philosopher* and many other Concretes

[1] Notably G. E. Moore, *Are Characteristics Universal or Particular?*, Arist. Soc. Supp. Vol. III (1923), pp. 100–2; and C. H. Langford, 'General propositions', *Mind* 1929.

[2] *Cat.* 10ª29–32.

[3] *Logick*, I.iv.5.

are *Substantives*, as well as *Folly*, *Knavery* and *Philosophy*, which are the abstract Terms that belong to them.'

Watts's account of this matter is reproduced in Mill[1] and Whately.[2] Mill (and Whately too, in a footnote) accompanies it with a polemic against a position which would seem to leave us with no 'concrete terms' but proper names. This view is that we must count every name as 'abstract' which we come to understand by a process of 'abstraction', i.e. by attending to some of the attributes of things and ignoring others. On this view 'white', for example, is as much an abstract term as 'whiteness', because the understanding of both involves attending to the whiteness of things in abstraction from their other qualities. Peirce[3] distinguishes at this point between 'precisive' or 'prescissive' abstraction, by which we think of a thing as, say, white, and ignore what else it is, and genuine or 'hypostatic' abstraction, by which we treat some feature of a thing as if it were itself a thing, or at all events an entity in its own right. It is only the latter sort of abstraction which leads us to form such words as 'whiteness', i.e. abstract terms in the sense of Watts, Whately and Mill. Peirce's word 'precisive' is derived from Watts, who, however, seems to apply it to the kind of abstraction which Peirce calls 'hypostatic', Peirce's 'prescission' being closer to what Watts calls 'negative' abstraction.[4]

The distinction between individual and general terms will be further investigated in the next chapter; but we may note here that the notion of a general term is to be distinguished not only from that of an abstract one, but also from that of a *collective* term, though some terms are both general and collective, just as some (like 'colour') are both general and abstract. A general term such as 'man' refers indifferently to any one of a number of individuals (it does so directly in such statements as 'I met a man the other day I

---

[1] *System*, I.ii.4.
[2] *Elements*, II.v.2.
[3] *Collected Papers*, 2.364, 428; 4.235, 332, 463.
[4] '*Precisive Abstraction*,' Watts says, 'is when we consider those Things apart which cannot really exist apart; as when we consider a *Mode*, without considering its *Substance* and *Subject* . . . *Negative Abstraction* is when we consider one Thing separate from another, which may also exist without it . . . If I think of *reading* or *writing* without the express Idea of some *Man*, this is *precisive Abstraction* . . . But when I think of a *Needle*, without an Idea of its *Sharpness*, this is *negative Abstraction*.'

3

never had met before', or 'Every man is mortal'; and a little less directly in such a statement as 'Man is the only animal gifted with intelligence'). A collective term, such as 'the Pyrenees', 'the British Army', 'the Canterbury College Council', refers to a group of individuals considered as a single totality. The examples just given are singular collective terms, but we also have terms such as 'army', 'regiment', 'mountain range', which refer indifferently to any one of a number of such collections, and so are general as well as collective. Sometimes, as has been noted in Part I, a phrase such as 'All the Peers' is used as a collective term; and sometimes, also, what appears to be a collective term is used distributively, as when we say 'The Council were all in favour of the motion', meaning that every member of the Council was in favour of it.

5. *The ten predicaments*

'Expressions which are in no way composite,' says Aristotle in the fourth chapter of the *Categories*, 'signify substance, quantity, quality, relation, place, time, position, state, action or affection. To sketch my meaning roughly, examples of substance are "man" or "the horse", of quantity, such terms as "two cubits long" or "three cubits long", of quality, such attributes as "white", "grammatical", "double", "half", "greater", fall under the category of relation; "in the market place", "in the Lyceum", under that of place; "yesterday", "last year", under that of time. "Lying", "sitting", are terms indicating position; "shod", "armed", state; "to lance", "to cauterize", action; "to be lanced", "to be cauterized", affection.'

Just what is Aristotle distinguishing here? Fundamentally, it would seem, the kinds of information which a predicate may convey about its subject. 'This is in the market-place' tells us where the thing is; 'This is taller than that', how it is related to something else. Sometimes Aristotle calls the categories 'kinds of being', and this may be understood in two ways. When we say 'Socrates is a man' and 'Socrates is in the market-place', the word 'is' seems to be used in different senses—'in the market-place' is not something that one can 'be' in the same sense as that in which one may 'be' a man, and to 'be' walking about seems to be a different kind of 'being' again. And also, as has been noted in an earlier section, the sense in which a substance or thing 'is' or exists is different from that in

which some quality of the thing 'is' or exists, and different again is
the sense in which a relation of the thing to something else 'is' or
exists.

Aristotle's ten categories are of different degrees of logical interest,
and we shall consider here only two or three of the more important
ones. Under the head of 'substance'[1] he distinguishes 'first substances', which are simply individual things such as 'this man', and
'second substances', which are kinds of things, like 'man'. Predicates
in all the other categories are 'accidents'. Roughly speaking, proper
nouns indicate 'first substances', common nouns indicate 'second
substances', and adjectives indicate accidents. But only roughly, for
'Socrates is a man' and 'Socrates is human' seem to say of Socrates
exactly the same thing, and the same predicate cannot be in two
categories at once. Aristotle's view seems to have been that behind
the linguistic distinction, and only imperfectly expressed by it,
there is an objective one, which I think we may conceive as follows:[2]
Common sense assumes that the qualities of a thing, and its behaviour, depend on two factors, namely the nature of the thing
itself, and the circumstances in which it is placed. Things of the
same nature or kind, we say, will appear and behave similarly in
similar circumstances but differently in different circumstances, and
things of different kinds will behave differently in the same circumstances. So the attributes which any given thing has at any given
time consist (a) of ones which are the joint effect of its nature and its
circumstances, and (b) of ones which actually go to *make up* its
'nature'. Those falling under (a) are 'accidents' of the thing, while
those falling under (b) constitute its 'essence' or 'substance'—its
'substantial form', as the Schoolmen often said. That a dog has
distemper, we would say, is in this sense an 'accident' of that dog;
it is due to its having been in the sort of situation in which that kind
of being contracts distemper; but that it is a dog, Aristotle would
have said, is just its nature—it happens to be that kind of being.
Modern biologists would not agree with Aristotle on the latter point
—they would say that its being the kind of animal it is depends on
the circumstances in which its ancestors were placed, the only
'nature' involved being the general 'nature' of living beings. And

---

[1] *Categories*, ch. 5.
[2] For a more detailed elaboration of the line of thought which follows, see
Broad's *Examination of McTaggart's Philosophy*, vol. 1, pp. 265–73.

we might in principle be able to explain that too as due to the circumstances in which the chemicals of which living organisms are composed have been placed. Chemists in their turn would not now regard the various elements as so many kinds of things whose 'nature' must simply be accepted as an ultimate fact. That too can in principle be explained by the situations in which the electrons, etc. are placed in the various kinds of atoms. There are arguments against these various reductions; but even if we put them aside, the Aristotelian distinction between substance (or nature) and accident has only been pushed from biology and chemistry into sub-atomic physics, and it is extremely questionable whether scientists will ever be able to do without it. For most of the purposes of formal logic, however, the distinction is unimportant. 'Socrates is coloured' follows equally cogently, and in the same way, from 'Every man is coloured, and Socrates is a man' and from 'Every white thing is coloured, and Socrates is white', though the middle term in the one case possibly signifies his substance or nature and in the other case only an accident.

What is predicated of a certain kind of thing may, then, be one of the attributes going to make up the essence or inner nature of that kind of thing, or it may be merely one of the attributes which a thing has come to possess (temporarily or permanently) through the situations in which it (being the kind of thing it is) has been placed. This is the difference between 'essential' and 'accidental' predication. If what is predicated makes up the whole inner nature of that of which it is predicated, it constitutes what Aristotle called the 'definition' of the subject. If it is only a part of the essence, and is shared by that kind of subject with other kinds, it is what Aristotle called its 'genus'.[1] Locke, better aware than Aristotle of the difficulty of being sure when we have reached the point when we must just say 'This kind of thing is the way it is because it is its nature to be so', said that in natural science at least we must be content to distinguish between what does and what does not belong to the 'nominal' essences of things.[2] That is, in practice we must divide things into classes, and give them general names, according to whether they possess or lack certain attributes which we pitch upon as making useful lines of division. The possession of these

[1] *Topics*, I.5.
[2] *Essay concerning Human Understanding*, III,vi,1–9.

attributes then becomes 'essential' to the applicability of these names, because we have made it so.

CHAPTER FOUR

The General Term

1. *General and singular terms in Whately and Mill*

A 'common term' (*terminus communis*) is defined in Peter of Spain's *Summulae*[1] as 'one of such a nature that it may be predicated of many' (*aptus natus est praedicari de pluribus*), as 'man' may be predicated of Socrates, of Plato, and of each and every particular man. A 'singular term' (*terminus singularis*), by contrast, is 'of such a nature that it may be predicated of one subject only' (*aptus natus est praedicari de uno solo*).[2] There is an obvious echo here of Aristotle's definition of a 'universal' in the *De Interpretatione*. Similar accounts of the distinction are given by later writers. 'It is evident,' says Whately,[3] 'that a proper-name, or any other term which denotes but a single individual, as "Caesar", "the Thames", "the Conqueror of Pompey", "this river" (hence called in Logic a "Singular-term") cannot be affirmed of any thing besides that individual . . . On the other hand, those terms which are called "*Common*", as denoting any one individual of a whole class, as "river", "conqueror", may of course be affirmed of any, or all that belong to that class.' And Mill:[4] 'A general name is familiarly defined, a name which is capable of being truly affirmed, in the same sense, of each of an indefinite number of things. An individual or singular name is a name which is only capable of being truly affirmed, in the same sense, of one thing.'

The reference in Mill's version of the definition to unambiguity of sense is necessary because the same proper name may be given to different individuals. In such a case each different application of the name constitutes a different 'meaning'; for as Johnson has expressed

[1] Bochenski's edition, 1.08.
[2] Ibid., 1.09.
[3] *Elements*, 1.6.
[4] *System*, 1.ii.3.

it,[1] what a proper name 'means' is identical with what it 'factually indicates'; but when a general name such as 'man' is applied to a number of different individuals, it is 'affirmed of all of them in the same sense'. An important consequence of this is that general names do *not* 'mean' the things they 'factually indicate', i.e. the individual things to which they are applicable; their 'meaning' lies elsewhere. How Mill elaborated this point we shall consider shortly. In Peter of Spain the distinction in question is described as one between *significatio* and *suppositio*. The 'signification' of a word is that reality to which custom has attached it; its 'supposition' is what we use it, with this signification, to stand for.[2] What the word 'man' signifies is a particular *kind* of thing; but in 'A man is running' the word does not stand for that kind of thing but for a particular thing of that kind—it is not a kind-of-thing that runs, but an individual.

According to medieval logic, the same term, without altering its signification, may have different suppositions in different contexts. Sometimes it does stand for (*supponit pro*) that which it means; in which case it has, in the terminology of the *Summulae*,[3] 'simple' supposition. Thus in 'Man is a species' it *is* a kind of thing that is being spoken of; no individual man is a species. But more usually the supposition of a common term, at least when it is subject, is 'personal', in which use it is not the kind, but individuals of the kind, which are being spoken of.[4] A modern logician would probably say that if there are such entities as 'kinds of things', and if 'man' in 'Man is a species' is the name of such an entity, then it is not being used as a general but as a singular term.

There are various theories as to what a general term 'means'. Perhaps it means, as the medieval logicians held, a 'kind of thing'; perhaps a 'class' of things; perhaps the attribute or set of attributes which marks off such a class. In none of these cases, we must repeat, does it 'mean' one of these entities in the sense of being applicable to it. The class of men is not the object, or one of the objects, of which we are speaking when we say 'Some men are liars', nor is the attribute of humanity—we do not mean that the class of men, or the attribute of humanity, is a liar; and when we want to speak of this

---

[1] *Logic*, I.vi.6.
[2] *Summulae* (Bochenski's edition), 6.03.
[3] Ibid., 6.05.
[4] Ibid., 6.08.

class or this attribute we do not speak of it as a man but use the appropriate word or phrase (as when we say 'The class of men has many members' or 'Humanity is a combination of rationality and animality'). But a general term *uses* a class or an attribute to refer to individuals.

Whately and Mill are particularly insistent that it is not the class but the attribute that is in this sense 'meant' by a general term. A 'class', for them, is essentially a derivative notion. To belong to a certain class, Whately says repeatedly, is simply to 'answer to' a certain 'description'. And 'it is evident that, in any case, we refer something to a certain Class *in consequence* of that thing's possessing certain attributes, and not *vice versa*'.[1] So also Mill, who says that the description of a general name as 'the name of a *class*' merely 'explains the clearer of two things by the more obscure', and that 'it would be more logical to reverse the proposition, and turn it into a definition of the word *class* "A class is the indefinite multitude of things denoted by a general name" ',[2] a general name bing 'a name . . . of all things . . . which possess certain definite attributes'.[3] Mill learnt this not only from Whately but from Thomas Reid, who laid it down that 'common names . . . signify common attributes'.[4]

Mill liked to express this doctrine by saying that general names like adjectives, are 'connotative'. 'A connotative term is one which denotes a subject, and implies an attribute . . . The word white, denotes all white things, as snow, paper, the foam of the sea, etc., and implies, or in the language of the Schoolmen, *connotes*, the attribute *whiteness*. The word white is not predicated of the attribute, but of the subjects, snow, etc.; but when we predicate it of them, we convey the meaning that the attribute whiteness belongs to them . . . All concrete general names are connotative. The word *man*, for example, denotes Peter, Jane, John, and an indefinite number of other individuals . . . But it is applied to them, because they possess, and to signify that they possess, certain attributes.'[5] Whether Mill has accurately reproduced the medieval use of the word 'connote' is an obscure point; but the doctrine he expresses

[1] *Elements*, I.3.
[2] *System*, I.ii.3.
[3] Ibid., I.v.3.
[4] *Essays on the Intellectual Powers*, v.vi.
[5] *System*, I.ii.5.

by it is clear enough. Whately uses 'connotative' in the same sense, but prefers 'attributive'. He says, 'When a term applied to some object is such as to imply in its signification some *"attribute"* belonging to that object, such a term is called by some of the early logical writers *"Connotative"*; but would perhaps be more conveniently called *"Attributive"* . . . Every Concrete-common-term is "attributive" (connotative), whether in the adjective or substantive form; as "Man", "human", "triangle", "triangular", "saint", "holy" for, "man" e.g. or "human", are appellations denoting, not the *attribute itself* which we call "human-nature", but a Being to which such a term is applied in reference to, and *by virtue of*, its possessing that attribute.'[1]

Mill sometimes expresses this point of view by saying that to apply a general name to an object is to convey information about it, in a way that giving it a proper name is not. This too he seems to have learnt from Reid, who is quoted to that effect in his *Examination of Hamilton's Philosophy*.[2] What Reid[3] says is that 'a proper name signifies nothing but the name of the individual whose name it is; and, when we apply it to the individual, we neither affirm nor deny anything concerning him', whereas when we 'apply the name of son or brother to several persons, this signifies and affirms that this attribute is common to all of them'. Mill has been much criticised for defending this doctrine, but his arguments are strong, and the criticisms seem for the most part based on misunderstandings which he does his best to obviate. He admits, for example, that when a proper name is assigned to a child, say, or a place, there may often have been some reason for selecting that name rather than any other; but argues that 'the name, once given, is independent of the reason', and will not cease to be applicable when the reason disappears. Dartmouth will not cease to be so called if it ceases, through some change in the course of the river, to be at the mouth of the Dart; its being so is therefore no part of the name's 'signification'.[4]

Mill admits also that beside proper names there are 'connotative individual names' which do convey information about the objects

[1] *Elements*, II.v.I.
[2] Ch. 17.
[3] Op. cit.
[4] *System*, I.ii.5.

which they denote. These are the terms which Lord Russell calls 'definite descriptions'; they are always complex, containing a general name with additions which in one way or another restrict its application to a single individual. Mill would not, therefore, have opposed Whately's contention that the singular term 'the founder of Rome' is attributive, the founding of Rome being, 'by that appellation, "*attributed*" to the person to whom it is applied'.[1] Such 'connotative individual names' are distinguished not only from proper names but also from names which merely happen—not in virtue of their meaning, but in virtue of how things are—to apply to one thing only. Such names as these, Mill says, are not really 'individual' names at all, but general ones. For although general names are traditionally defined as being predicable in principle of a plurality of objects, we must not understand by this that a name is only to be accounted general if there are in fact a plurality of objects to which it truly applies. The older commentators on the definition made this plain too; Whately is only echoing them when, before defining a common term as one 'denoting any one individual of a whole class', he indicates that 'by "*Class*" is meant throughout this treatise, not merely a "Head" or "general description" to which several things are *actually* referred, but one to which an indefinite number of things *might conceivably* by referred; viz. as many as (in the colloquial phrase) may "*answer to the description*" . . . When then anything is said to be "*referred to such a Class*", this is to be understood either of an *actual*, or what may be called a *potential* Class: i.e. the word Class is used whether these actually exist, or not, *several* things to which a description may apply.'[2] And Mill goes further— a general name, he says, may have a perfectly definite meaning, and so be a genuine general name, even if there is nothing at all to which it applies. Not only may we 'frame a class without knowing the individuals, or any of the individuals, of which it may be composed', but 'we may do so while believing that no such individuals exist'.[3]

Another admission that Mill makes in discussing the non-connotativeness of proper names is that in referring to things by proper names we may put the hearer in mind of a great deal that he

[1] *Elements*, II.v.i.
[2] Ibid., 1.3.
[3] *System*, I.v.3.

already thinks or knows about them. 'By enabling him to identify the individuals, we may connect them with information previously possessed by him; by saying, This is York, we may tell him that it contains the Minster. But this is in virtue of what he has previously heard concerning York, not by anything implied in the name.' We 'understand' the use of a proper name if we know to what individual it applies; that, therefore, is strictly what it means, and all that it means. On the other hand, if we know nothing about a general name except what individuals it applies to, we do *not* know its meaning, and we may know its meaning without knowing that.[1] Moreover, though the meaning of a general name does lie in a set of attributes, a general name as well as a proper one may 'put us in mind' of attributes that are no part of its meaning, but that we happen to know are found in the objects to which the name applies. Mill emphasises this point in dealing with Brown's theory that the conclusion of a syllogism follows from its minor premiss alone— that 'the proposition, Socrates is mortal, is evolved from the proposition, Socrates is a man, simply by recognising the notion of mortality as already contained in the notion we form of a man'. This would only be so, Mill says, if being mortal were part of the connotation of 'man'; but in fact, as the word is ordinarily used, it is not. He distinguishes here between 'the idea of man, as a universal idea', i.e. the set of attributes which common usage has settled upon as determining the applicability of the name, and a person's 'private idea of man', in which he will always include other attributes beside these (of which mortality may be one), but 'only as the consequence of experience; . . . so that whatever the idea contains, in any person's mind, beyond what is included in the conventional signification of the word, has been added to it as the result of assent to a proposition', which proposition requires to be explicitly stated for the syllogistic conclusion to be validly drawn.[2]

Mill does, however, agree with Brown—as Whately before him had agreed with the eighteenth-century critics of the syllogism—that the examples of syllogisms given in the older Logic-books often use premisses which really have the superfluous character mistakenly attributed by Brown to 'All men are mortal'—premisses which attribute to the subject a character which is already included among

[1] Ibid., I.ii.5.
[2] Ibid., II.iii.6.

those which make up its very meaning.[1] Such a proposition, which 'asserts of a thing under a particular name only what is asserted of it in the fact of calling it by that name', Mill was in the habit of describing as 'merely verbal'; and it was his belief that all the propositions which Aristotle and the Schoolmen called 'essential' were in fact of that character. He believed, in other words, that Locke's 'nominal essences' are the only 'essences' there are; that to say, for example, that it is of the essence of Man to be rational, is just to say that it is not our custom to apply the word 'man' to beings that lack rationality; and that 'All men are rational' is therefore true, not because of any profound fact of nature, but simply because we have so chosen to use the word 'man' that the proposition is an 'identical' one, meaning 'All rational Xs are rational' (where 'X' stands for the remainder of the conditions that must be satisfied before the description 'human' can be considered applicable). In such cases, 'the universal affirmative proposition will be true' simply because 'whatever possesses the whole of any set of attributes, must possess any part of that same set'.[2]

Mill identifies his distinction between 'verbal' and 'real' propositions not only with the scholastic one between 'essential' and 'accidental' predication, but also with Kant's distinction between 'analytic' (or 'explicative') and 'synthetic' (or 'ampliative') propositions or judgements. Kant calls the judgement that bodies are extended an 'analytic' one, and the judgement that bodies are heavy a 'synthetic' one, because extension is one of the properties we must think of an object as having in order to think of it as a body, whereas heaviness is not. Mill takes this (whether he does so rightly has been disputed) to mean that extension is, and heaviness is not, one of the attributes which a thing must have before we will consent to apply the term 'body' to it; and in his *Examination of Hamilton's Philosophy*[3] he connects this distinction with that which he makes in his criticism of Brown on the syllogism. Hamilton held the view that (expressing it in Mill's words) 'a judgment is a recognition in thought, a proposition a statement in words, that one notion is or is not a part of another'. But this, Mill argues, simply does away with the distinction between analytic and synthetic judgements by

[1] Cf. Whately's *Elements*, Intro., 4, and IV.ii.1; and Mill's *System*, I.vi.4.
[2] *System*, I.vi.2.
[3] Ch. 18.

making them all analytic. Or if we take account of another doctrine sometimes put forward by Hamilton, that when a judgement is first made it constitutes the *incorporating* of the predicate-notion in the subject-notion, his view would 'compel him to maintain that all judgments which are not new are analytical, and that synthetical judgments are limited to truths, or supposed truths, which we learn for the first time'. It is interesting that this position, which Mill saw as a logical consequence of Hamilton's view of judgement, was later seriously held by Bradley, who argued that 'a synthetic judgment, so soon as it is made, is at once analytic'. The source of the whole trouble, Mill says, lies in the fact that 'the concept of a class, in Sir W. Hamilton's acceptation of the term, includes all the attributes which we have judged, and still judge, to be common to the whole class. It means, in short, our entire knowledge of the class'. To make possible the distinction between analytic and synthetic, 'concepts must be so construed as to consist of those attributes only which are connoted by the name', i.e. without which we would refuse to apply it.

It is a consequence of Mill's account of essential predication, and of his account of proper names, that propositions with a proper name as subject-term can never be 'essential'.[1] We can never attribute to a subject so referred to part or all of what is already attributed to it in so referring to it; for nothing at all is attributed to it in so referring to it. 'Merely verbal' propositions of another sort can, however, be constructed with a proper name as subject-term, namely ones with another proper name as predicate, as in 'Tully is Cicero'. This, Mill argues, merely tells us that 'both the names are marks for the same object'.[2] He discusses this case in connection with a theory of Hobbes's which amounts to treating all propositions whatever as being of the same sort as this one. What Hobbes says is that all propositions simply tell us that things referred to by one name are or are not among the things referred to by another. Mill's principal argument against this is that, by concentrating on the denotation of names and ignoring their connotation, it takes no account of *why* the names are applicable to the objects in question. Certainly if all men are mortal then the word 'mortal' is applicable to anything to which the word 'man' is applicable, but only because wherever the

[1] *System*, I.vi.3.
[2] Ibid., I.v.2.

attributes which entitle a thing to be called a 'man' are found the attribute which entitles us to call it 'mortal' is found also; and this fact about the attributes, rather than the derived fact about the names, is what 'All men are mortal' asserts.

This is the theory of the 'import' of propositions which Mill pits against both Hobbes and Hamilton. In the case of 'real' propositions with proper names as subjects, what is asserted is 'that the individual thing denoted by the subject, has the attributes connoted by the predicate'. And something of the same sort is true up to a point of propositions in which the subject is general. Here too the proposition asserts that 'the objects denoted by the subject . . . possess the attributes connoted by the predicate'. But in this case 'the objects are no longer *individually* designated. They are pointed out only by some of their attributes.' In 'All men are mortal', therefore, what is asserted 'is not . . . that the attributes which the predicate connotes are possessed by any given individual, or by any number of individuals previously known as John, Thomas, etc., but that those attributes are possessed by each and every individual possessing certain other attributes.'[1] It means that 'the attributes of man are always accompanied by the attribute mortality'. The practical use of such a proposition is that it enables us, 'when we see or learn that an object possesses one of the two attributes, to infer that it possesses the other'. We might therefore say that what 'All men are mortal' means is that 'the attributes of men are *evidence of*, are a *mark* of, mortality'.[2] Mill proposed in this connection a substitute for the *Dictum de Omni*, which (in the form 'Whatever can be affirmed of a class, may be affirmed of everything included in it') he thought too liable to suggest that in syllogism we are just repeating ourselves—saying of every object in a certain list that it is Y, and then saying that X is Y because it is in the list.[3] His substitute, for syllogisms with singular minors, is 'Whatever has any mark, has that which it is a mark of', and with universal minors, 'A mark of any mark is a mark of that which this last is a mark of' (*Nota notae est nota rei ipsius*).[4]

One other point which Mill touches upon deserves mention—the

[1] *System*, I.v.4.
[2] Ibid., I.vi.5.
[3] Ibid., II.ii.2.
[4] *System*, II.ii.4; *Examination of Hamilton*, ch. 19.

connotation of 'infinite' terms such as 'not-man', 'not-tree', etc.[1]
While dissenting from Hobbes's view that what appears to be negative predication is always the affirmative predication of a negative
term, Mill appears to hold that the affirmative predication of a
negative term is something which may occur, and he says that 'when
the positive name is connotative, the corresponding negative name
is connotative likewise; but in a peculiar way, connoting not the
presence but the absence of an attribute'. This is puzzling, as it
suggests that positive names connote, not an attribute, but the
presence of an attribute, which would seem to be another attribute.
On the denotation of such names, Mill is clearer: '*not-white* denotes
all things whatever except white things'. In a footnote he contests
the view of Bain that 'negative names are not names of all things
denoted by the correlative positive name, but only for all things of
some particular class', applying 'not-white', for instance, only to
'every *coloured* thing other than white'.[2] On such a view, colour at
least would be connoted by 'not-white' in the ordinary way. Mill's
reply is that 'the test of what a name denotes is what it can be
predicated of: and we can certainly predicate of a sound, or a smell,
that it is not white. The affirmation and the negation of an
attribute cannot but divide the whole field of predication between
them.'

2. *General and singular terms in Keynes*
Part I of Keynes's *Formal Logic*, on 'Terms', is essentially a
systematisation, and on the whole a defence, of the body of doctrine
just outlined. His most noteworthy addition to it is simply the
association of distinct technical terms with the distinctions made by
Mill in his defence of the non-connotativeness of proper names. In
writers who speak in this part of Logic of 'concepts' or 'ideas' rather
than of terms or names, the set of objects associated with a concept
is generally called its 'extension', and the set of attributes which
constitute the concept itself is called its 'intension' or 'comprehension'. ('Extension' and 'comprehension' are used in the *Port-
Royal Logic*, and were favoured in Mill's day by Hamilton.) But in
these writers, as we have seen, it is not clear what attributes are

[1] *System*, I.ii.6 and n.
[2] Similar views have been propounded by other writers, such as Lotze. See,
on this subject, Joseph's *Introduction*, 2nd ed., pp. 40–6.

thought of as constituting a concept, i.e. as its 'intension'. What Keynes suggests is, first, that the term 'intension' be used as a generic one for the various ranges of attributes that might be considered in connection with a general name, the term 'connotation' being confined, as Mill confined it, to the 'conventional' intension or set of attributes which we employ (having possibly listed them in a formal definition) to determine whether an object is entitled to the name or not. Once this is fixed, those objects which possess the attributes will form the 'denotation' or 'objective extension' of the name, and those which do not will fall outside it. It is 'objective' because although we may arbitrarily select the attributes that will make up the connotation, what objects possess those attributes is a fact of nature which we do not decide but discover. These objects will in general have many other attributes in common beside those in virtue of which the name is applicable to them; the totality of such common properties, Keynes suggests, should be called the 'comprehension' or 'objective intension' of the name. There are, again, the various attributes 'called to mind' in various hearers when the name is uttered; these Keynes describes as forming the name's 'subjective' intension. This terminology first appears in his second edition[1] (in his first[2] he merely echoes Mill's insistence that the connotation of a class-name does not include all the attributes associated with it); in his third,[3] he makes an interesting addition to it. He points out that there is another way of fixing the meaning of a general name besides actually listing the characters which are to determine its applicability. We might, instead, indicate a set of objects (or of classes already defined) and say 'Whatever possesses all the common properties of those, I shall call an X'. A set of objects used in this way to fix the meaning of a name, Keynes calls its 'exemplification' or 'conventional extension'. Once such a set of objects has been fixed upon, the totality of their common characters will form the 'comprehension' of the name, and the totality of objects possessing all these characters will be its denotation. In the actual growth of a language there tends to be a continual alternation between these methods of fixing the meaning of words, and only with technical terms is any attempt made to fix it precisely. What

[1] §13.
[2] §13.
[3] §13 (4th ed., §22).

Whewell calls 'definition by type',[1] e.g. defining a rose as what resembles a selected group of specimens more than it resembles any other group (with, it may be presumed, as much diversity within it as the group selected), approximates to Keynes's 'extensive definition' or definition by exemplification. Reid too notes that in practice we learn the meaning of common words by 'a kind of induction', observing in what cases they are applied and in what they are not.[2] Instead of being told that anything that has such and such attributes may be called an X, and arguing 'This has the attributes, therefore we may call it an X', we are told 'That is called an X, and that, and that', and argue 'But all these things have such-and-such attributes, therefore anything that has them must be what is called an X'. It is only after we have come by some such process to use words in an approximately uniform manner that we find it convenient in technical contexts to restrict the meaning of some word to what possesses a certain named set of attributes.

It is plain that proper names have what Keynes calls 'subjective intension'; what they lack is, as Mill says, conventional connotation. Keynes says[3] that they are defined extensively, though this is a slightly different sort of 'extensive definition' from his 'exemplification'. (In giving a proper name to a thing, we are not treating it as a type or example.) Johnson[4] describes the process of establishing an association between a particular thing and its proper name as 'ostensive' definition (definition by showing) or 'introduction'.

It is plain also that if the fact that the things answering to a certain name possess a certain property is at all familiar, that property will be apt to enter into its 'subjective intension'; but this will not abolish the distinction between analytic and synthetic propositions, which remains fixed so long as the conventional connotation of the name is unaltered. Keynes is, however, more aware than Mill that we do from time to time alter the connotation of the words we use, and that this will alter the point at which the line between analytic and synthetic is drawn. If we use the word 'man'

---

[1] *Novum Organon Renovatum*, bk. I, aphorisms XCII, XCIII; bk. III, ch. III, arts. 14, 15. Whewell's views on this point are discussed in Mill's *System*, IV.vii.3–4.

[2] *Essays on the Intellectual Powers*, V.ii.

[3] *Formal Logic*, 4th ed., §24.

[4] *Logic*, I.vi.7.

as an abbreviation for 'animal capable of speech', 'Men are capable
of speech' will be analytic and 'Men are capable of using tools'
synthetic; while if we use it as an abbreviation for 'animal capable
of using tools', the reverse will be the case. But here, Keynes points
out,[1] our sentences cease to express the same propositions. Light is
also thrown on the distinction between analytic and synthetic by
Keynes's notion of 'extensive definition'. If we define a 'horse' as
anything with all the common properties of a certain set of objects
(and this is broadly how we do learn to use such words), then the
assertion that horses, let us say, have hooves, cannot be analytic,
for it will express the fact of nature that these objects all have
hooves. But a zoologist who has learnt this fact may decide that
having hooves would be a useful attribute to use as a *test* for the
applicability of the word 'horse' in his own technical sense of it;
and as *he* uses 'horse', 'Horses have hooves' will be analytic. On the
other hand, 'These objects are horses' will never be analytic when
'horse' is used in his sense, as it would be if the objects referred to
were some or all of those used to fix the meaning of the word.[2]

Keynes follows Mill in identifying the distinction between
'analytic' and 'synthetic' with that between 'verbal' and 'real', and
is not entirely free from some of the confusions into which Mill
falls on this subject. These confusions are all due to a failure on
Mill's part to distinguish carefully between (a) actually using a
certain word in a certain way, (b) stating that that is the way the
word is in fact used or going to be used, and (c) proposing to use the
word in that way. Thus he says that definitions are verbal propositions, and that for this reason they are incapable of truth or
falsity.[3] But the real reason why at least some definitions are not
capable of truth or falsity is not that they are about words but that,
as Whately saw,[4] and in our own time Johnson,[5] they are not in the
indicative but the imperative mood—they amount to saying 'Let us
use the word X to mean such-and-such'. The statement that such-
and-such is the common usage is as 'real' a proposition as any, in

---

[1] *Formal Logic*, 4th ed., §32. The opponent that Keynes has in mind is not
Hamilton but Bradley.

[2] Cf. Keynes, op. cit., p. 51, n. 2; and see the discussion in Broad's *Examination
of McTaggart*, vol. I, pp. 111–20.

[3] *System*, I.vi.1.

[4] *Elements*, II.v.6.

[5] *Logic*, I.iv.2.

the sense of being capable of truth or falsity. It is also 'real' in the sense of not being tautological. On the other hand, the actual use of a word in the sense proposed or described may cause a certain sentence to express a tautology; for example, using 'man' as an abbreviation for 'rational animal' will cause the sentence 'Men are rational' to express the tautology that what is both rational and animal is rational. As Reginald Jackson has made abundantly clear in his *Deductive Logic of J. S. Mill*,[1] Mill never clearly distinguishes between 'Man is rational' as used to express the tautology that rational animals are rational, and 'Man is rational' as used to convey the information that being rational is part of what the word 'man' is commonly used to mean. The same confusion leads him to assent to Hobbes's statement that sentences like 'All men are mortal' are used to express propositions about the use of the words 'man' and 'mortal' (while denying Hobbes's further contention that they express no more than this). Keynes too uses Mill's expression 'verbal proposition' in this ambiguous way; but he takes a long step towards clarification by distinguishing verbal propositions from what he calls 'formal' ones, which are so far from being true solely in virtue of the meaning of their terms that they are true no matter what the meaning of their terms may be.[2] 'Any rational animal is rational', expressed in that way, is in this sense a formal proposition; it would be just as true as it now is if 'rational' meant what we now mean by 'sticky' and 'animal' what we now mean by 'steering-wheel'. In point of fact there are no propositions which are true solely because of what their terms mean; propositions described in this way by Mill and others are really propositions which are true because, their terms meaning what they do mean, the propositions are merely formal.

Various other 'stock problems' find their solution in Keynes's distinction of the various forms of intension and extension. He examines, for example, the senses in which it is true that the intension and extension of a term vary inversely as one another.[3] The most important sense is just this, that if we add to the list of

[1] Ch. 5.

[2] *Formal Logic*, 4th ed., §31.

[3] This doctrine is hinted at in Aristotle—Joseph (*Introduction*, 2nd ed., p. 136) cites the *Physics* 210ª17–19—and is clearly enunciated in the *Port Royal Logic*, I.V.

attributes which an object must possess before we will consent to call it by a certain name, the number of objects passing our test, i.e. the number of objects possessing all the attributes in our list, will usually be lessened; though it will remain unaltered if the additions to our list happen to be characters already possessed by all the objects possessing those on our original list, and in any case no exact numerical relation between the increase and the decrease can be given. Objections to the 'inverse variation' doctrine are almost invariably based on the confusion between connotation and subjective intension. Not entirely, however; for the kind of change in connotation which tends to result in a decrease of denotation is not always a simple addition of characters to a list. We might, for example, first decide to apply a certain term to objects if they are, among other things, blue, and we may later stiffen the criterion by replacing 'blue' by 'ultramarine'; but to be ultramarine, as Johnson in effect points out in his chapter on 'The Determinable',[1] is not to be blue *and* something else besides, but is a particular way of being blue.

Keynes also considers exhaustively the various ways in which the terms of a proposition may be 'read'.[2] We may, for example, take 'All men are mortal' (as Mill took it) to mean that the attributes connoted by the predicate always accompany the attributes connoted by the subject. With both terms thus 'read in connotation', the proposition might be most appropriately expressed as 'Whatever is human is mortal'. Or we may take it to mean that the objects denoted by the subject possess the attributes connoted by the predicate, this being what is most naturally expressed by the form 'Every man is mortal'. Or we may take it to mean that the objects denoted by the subject are among the objects denoted by the predicate, the proper form for this being 'Every man is *a* mortal'. Since what is denoted by a term is simply what possesses the attributes connoted by it, these interpretations are equivalent; and from any of them, but most obviously from the last, it follows that the attributes making up the comprehension of the predicate are among the attributes making up the comprehension of the subject, i.e. that whatever is true of every mortal is true of every man.

On the connotation of negative terms, Keynes takes the view that

[1] *Logic*, i.xi.3. Cf. Cook Wilson, *Statement and Inference*, vol. i, 155–60.
[2] *Formal Logic*, pt. ii, ch. 6.

it is in each case the same as that of the corresponding positive term, but the relation of connotation to denotation, and so the denotation itself, is different. 'Regarding *not-A* . . . as equivalent to *whatever is not A*, we may say that its justification and explanation is to be found primarily by reference to the *extension* of the name. The thinking of anything as *A* involves its being distinguished from that which is not *A*. Thus on the extensive side every concept divides the universe . . . into two mutually exclusive subdivisions, namely, a portion of which *A* can be predicated and a portion of which *A* cannot be predicated. These we designate *A* and *not-A* respectively. While it may be said that *A* and *not-A* involve *intensively* only one concept, they are *extensively* mutually exclusive.'[1] Like Mill, he rejects Bain's view that in a term like 'not-A' there is always a reference to some more indefinite attribute (like colour, where A = 'white') which things that are not A share with things that are. He admits that ordinarily the things we are considering in making any given predication are tacitly limited to what he calls a 'universe of discourse' (in contrasting what is white with what is not, for example, it is generally only coloured things and not sounds or virtues that we have in mind); but he insists that there is no reason in principle why this 'universe of discourse' should not be as wide as we care to make it.[2]

3. *General and singular terms in Johnson, Peirce and Frege*

In his discussion of the 'import' of propositions, Mill's main point is that what we have to understand about a general term in order to understand a proposition in which it occurs (whether as predicate or as subject) is what attributes it connotes—what objects it may denote, is immaterial. But connected with this is a subsidiary contention, namely that the connection between the meanings of its terms which a proposition asserts, is not (except in a few peculiar instances) one of identity, nor even that of part and whole. Where the subject is singular, what is asserted is that the predicate-attribute is present in it, not as a part in a whole, but in the indefinable way in which attributes are present in subjects; where it is general, that the subject-attributes are always accompanied by the predicate-attribute. This contention might also be expressed by saying that

[1] *Formal Logic*, 4th ed., §38.
[2] Ibid., §39.

the fundamental form of predication is not (as some accounts of 'logical form' would suggest that it is) that in which both subject and predicate appear as nouns, but rather that in which the predicate appears as an adjective, and the subject either as a proper noun or as the adjectival predicate of a subordinate clause. 'Socrates is human' is not just a lazy way of saying that Socrates is a human-thing or man, for the notion of being human is presupposed in that of being a man—a man is just a thing that is human. Adjectives are so far from being 'syncategorematic', mere parts of 'terms' in the proper sense, that they are the most proper way for a predicate-term, and indeed for any general term, to be expressed. The only common noun that is essential is the indefinite 'thing'—all common nouns, one might say, are reducible to the noun 'thing' with an adjectival qualification, just as the traditional account of 'logical form' reduces all verbs to the one verb 'is' with an adjectival complement.

Mill's point of view is elaborated and defended in these terms in Part I of Johnson's *Logic*. What is asserted in the simplest type of proposition, Johnson holds, is that some adjective characterises some substantive (where 'adjective' and 'substantive' are used not for kinds of words but for kinds of entities which words may signify) not that certain substantives are identical. Nothing is gained, therefore, by transforming 'Socrates is mortal' into 'Socrates is (identical with) a mortal being'. For this translation leaves unexplained the force of the 'is' in 'is identical with' (if it too means identity, we have an infinite regress), and also leaves unexplained the relation between 'mortal' and 'being' in the new predicate—a relation which in fact must itself be expressed by 'is', 'mortal being' meaning 'being that is mortal'. So this expansion itself presupposes the relation between a thing and its characters expressed by 'is' in the original form 'Socrates is mortal'.[1]

Even to call this a relation, moreover, is in some ways a little misleading. For we can do with 'is characterised by', in 'Socrates is characterised by mortality', or in 'Socrates is characterised by identity with something that is characterised by mortality', exactly what Johnson does with 'is identical with'. What is the force of the 'is' in 'is characterised by'? If it expresses characterisation, we would seem to be again involved in an infinite regress. There is a

[1] *Logic*, I.i.6.

hint of this in Plato's criticism of his own theory of 'forms' in the *Parmenides*,[1] and more than a hint of it in Bradley's attack on the whole notion of different things being related to one another by real relations. (There must then, Bradley says, be further relations to relate each related thing to the relation which relates it to the other, and so on *ad infinitum*.) Johnson's answer to this in the *Logic*[2] is that 'is' does not strictly speaking represent the relation of characterisation but what he calls the 'characterising *tie*'. This is not an additional element beside substantive and adjective which enters into the structure of propositions; it is rather what Professor Broad[3] calls the 'form of union' of the constructed proposition.

In *The Logical Calculus*[4] this point is expressed by a more radical revision of the theory that propositions are ideally expressed with both terms as nouns. Here there is what amounts to a 'first draft' of the argument about 'Socrates is mortal' in the later work, but what is given as the least misleading form of singular proposition is not even the noun–copula–adjective form but the original Platonic and early-Aristotelian noun and verb. The 'singular substantive' is the 'subject-term' and the 'finite verb' the 'predicative-term'. The copula is superfluous. Predication by means of the verb is presupposed in the use of adjectives and common nouns alike. In 'Socrates is mortal', 'the predicate-term mortal . . . is a name given to any individual of whom mortality can be predicated', i.e. of whom we may say, 'He *must die*'. As for the substantival predicate of 'Socrates is *a* mortal', 'it is true that, starting with the conception of "dying", we may proceed to form the conception of the class of individuals which contains all who must die and no others. But this class is defined by means of predication thus: "Whoever must die." It is obviously circuitous to interpret the proposition "Socrates must die" to mean "Socrates is-identical-with one or other of those who must die".' If we try to get rid of the remaining 'must die' in the same way, we only repeat 'are-identical-with one or other of those who' interminably. And 'is-identical-with' is itself a verb too;

---

[1] See G. Ryle, 'Plato's *Parmenides*', *Mind* 1939, pp. 137–40; also J. Anderson, ' "Universals" and Occurrences', *Australasian Journal of Psychology and Philosophy*, June 1929.

[2] I.xiii.5.

[3] *Examination of McTaggart's Philosophy*, vol. I, p. 94.

[4] First article II.

'Tully is Cicero', in the sense of 'Tully is-identical-with Cicero', is logically on a par with 'Brutus loves Caesar'. To sum up: we do not explain the functioning of the verb in a proposition by equating it with the functioning of a common noun or adjective linked by 'is' to the subject; rather, we explain the functioning of common nouns and adjectives in propositions by equating it with the functioning of a verb.

This point of view reflects the influence upon Johnson (at this stage) of the writings of C. S. Peirce. It was one of Peirce's favourite contentions that common nouns and adjectives are superfluous parts of speech, and that all the work they do can be done more straightforwardly by means of verbs.[1] He was in the habit of under-lining the predicative character of verbs and verbal phrases by representing them with a dash to indicate the point at which a subject was required, thus: '— is a mortal', '— is mortal', '— must die'. He used this device primarily in his development of the logic of relations; his view there is the now familiar one, that relative terms are verbs which require more than one subject to make a complete sentence. (He therefore represented them thus: '— loves —'; '— is a teacher of —'; '— is superior to —'; '— gives — to —').[2] Predicates thus conceived as propositions with their subjects left out he called 'rhemes', from the Greek for 'verb'. A typical maxim of his was that 'a term is a proposition whose subjects have had their denotative force removed'.[3] What this suggests is a form of speech such as 'This must die', where 'This' is not accom-panied by any demonstrative gesture. We would commonly describe such a form of speech as a proposition or sentence, but it is not really one until the 'this' has been given 'denotative force' in the usual way—until then it is not a proposition but rather a term, a predicate waiting for its subject. And all terms, Peirce sometimes says, are really of this kind. More often he excepts proper names and especially demonstrative pronouns, i.e. the kinds of 'terms' which may fill the blanks in 'rhemes' but which are not 'rhemes' themselves; but he speaks too of 'the impotence of mere words . . . to fulfil the functions of a grammatical subject',[4] and he seems some-

[1] See, e.g., *Collected Papers*, 2.328, 3.459.
[2] Ibid., 3.461, 465, 636.
[3] Ibid., 2.356.
[4] Ibid., 3.419.

times to think of the gesture which fixes the reference of a demonstrative pronoun as a kind of copula attaching the entire
proposition as predicate to the thing indicated as subject. The fact
that 'our word "*is*," the copula, is commonly expressed in Old
Egyptian by a demonstrative pronoun',[1] fascinated him.

Associated in Peirce with this view of terms, at all events of
general terms, as eviscerated propositions, is a similar view of
propositions as eviscerated inferences. 'A proposition is nothing
more nor less than an argumentation whose propositions have had
their assertiveness removed.'[2] He has in mind here what happens
when we replace the inference 'Every man is mortal, therefore every
good man is mortal' by the conditional proposition 'If every man
is mortal then every good man is mortal', where the component
propositions have ceased to be categorically asserted. Peirce's
attempt to meet the objection that this applies only to conditionals
by arguing that all propositions are conditional at bottom, is not
convincing. But he was attracted to the view that the distinction
between terms, propositions and arguments is of no logical importance—logic studies inter-relations and forms of composition which
we may encounter equally in any of these three fields.[3] (This is of a
piece with his refusal to make any distinction between the Logic
of Hypotheticals and the Logic of Categoricals.) He does at least
make good his subsidiary contention that the relation between a
term and a proposition and that between a proposition and an
argument are not themselves merely forms of composition; for his
examples show that the composition of terms may just as easily
produce another term as a proposition, and the composition of
propositions may just as easily produce another proposition as an
argument.

Peirce's view of quantified propositions is obscure—sometimes[4] he
describes quantifiers as 'instructions' for finding a subject—but
where what would ordinarily be called the subject-term is descriptive in character, he throws it into the predicate, making 'Every
man is mortal' for example, an assertion that no matter what subject
you choose to take, the complex rheme 'if — is a man then — is

[1] 2.354.
[2] 2.356.
[3] 4.572.
[4] As in 2.330.

mortal' may be truly predicated of it. This is Johnson's procedure also,[1] and in substance that of *Principia Mathematica*. As to negative terms, Peirce's system practically eliminates the distinction between affirmative propositions with negative predicates, and negative propositions; for a negative predicate is just a negative proposition with the subject left out. (And negative subjects, like all other subjects except proper names and demonstratives, may be thrown into the predicate.)

The 'noun-verb' analysis of non-compound propositions has received its most systematic elaboration at the hands of Frege.[2] Frege makes a radical distinction between what he calls 'objects' and what he calls 'concepts'. This is not a distinction between the mental and the non-mental, as if 'concepts' were somehow in the mind and 'objects' outside of it. The difference is rather that an object is anything that can be *named*, i.e. referred to by what Frege calls a 'proper name', while a concept can only be indicated by a predicative expression. 'Proper names', for Frege, include all singular terms—'this man' or 'the man next door' as well as 'Jones'. To refer to concepts he indifferently uses verbs, adjectives and common nouns, and expressions grammatically equivalent to these. On the whole he favours the common noun, contrasting the concept referred to by 'man' with the object referred to by 'this man'; and he would say that 'Socrates is a man' asserts that the object Socrates 'falls under' the concept referred to by 'man', or more briefly, the concept 'man'. A fundamental feature of his theory is that objects can never function as concepts, nor concepts as objects, though an object may function as part of a concept, and a concept as part of an object. There are various apparent exceptions to this, and Frege disposes of these with great skill and subtlety.

Objects apparently functioning as concepts are dismissed without much difficulty, though in the course of their dismissal some important distinctions are made. The planet Venus is unquestionably an object; but in 'The morning star is Venus', the morning star might

[1] *Logical Calculus*, 1st article, §17; *Logic*, 1.ix.2.

[2] For what follows, the main source is Frege's article 'On Concept and Object' (1892), translated by P. T. Geach in *Mind*, April 1951, together with the passages in *The Foundations of Arithmetic* to which it refers. [This article has now been reprinted in *Philosophical Writings of Gottlob Frege*, ed. P. Geach and M. Black, Oxford 1953.] Mr Geach's own article, 'Subject and Predicate' (*Mind*, October 1950), is also useful reading here.

appear to be put under the concept of Venus in the same way as it is put under the concept of a planet in 'The morning star is a planet'. Here Frege simply distinguishes between the 'is' of predication and the 'is' of identity. In 'The morning star is Venus', he says, 'is' is not a mere sign of predication, but means 'is no other than'; so it is not the concept of Venus but the concept of being no other than Venus that is predicated. (There is, in fact, no 'concept of Venus'.) It is true that the concept of being no other than Venus has only one object that falls under it, but the concept and the object are nevertheless distinct. (Lord Russell writes sometimes as if this were a discovery of Frege's, but the distinction is already quite clearly present in the traditional insistence that a general name is none the less general when there happens to be only one object to which it is truly applicable.) The object Venus is nevertheless a part of the concept of being no other than Venus (besides being the only object falling under it); at all events, the proper name 'Venus' is part of the predicative phrase '(is) no other than Venus'.

There are also cases in which concepts appear to function as objects. The easiest of these to deal with are the so-called 'subject-concepts' of general propositions such as 'All mammals have red blood'. Here, as Frege says, the essentially predicative function of the word 'mammals' may be brought out by transforming the whole into 'Whatever is a mammal has red blood', or 'If anything is a mammal it has blood'. Nor does the combination 'All mammals' refer to an object, as the combination 'This mammal' would do. For if it did, we would deny the proposition by saying 'All mammals are not-red-blooded' (i.e. 'No mammals are red-blooded') just as we would deny 'This mammal is red-blooded' by saying 'This mammal is not red-blooded'. But we do not in fact form the contradictory of 'All mammals are red-blooded' that way—we deny it by attaching the 'not' to the 'all', and saying 'Not all mammals are red-blooded'. This, Frege says, shows that 'all' is not part of the subject of this proposition, but part of its predicate. But what *is* its predicate, and of what is it predicated? Frege says that in such a proposition we put a first-level concept under a second-level one; specifically we put the first-level concept referred to by 'mammal' or 'is a mammal' under the second-level concept referred to by the rest of the sentence, i.e. by 'Every . . . is red-blooded' or by 'Everything that . . . is red-blooded'. This is where his difficulties begin.

Frege carefully distinguishes between the notion of a first-level concept 'falling under' a second-level one and the notion of a concept being 'subordinate' to another concept of the same 'level' as itself. The concept 'whale' is subordinate to the concept 'mammal' in the sense that anything falling under the former falls under the latter. But that is not to say that the concept 'while' itself falls under the concept 'mammal', i.e. is a mammal. It does mean, however, that the concept 'whale' falls under the concept 'subordinate to the concept "mammal"'. And does not this mean that the concept of being a whale functions here as an object? Frege answers this by what is the hardest of all his hard sayings. The concept of being a whale, he says, *is* an object; and for that very reason the concept of being a whale is not a concept. He would equally say that the concept referred to by the predicate 'is a whale' is not a concept but an object. In fact, anything whatever that is referred to by a phrase beginning 'The concept . . .' is not a concept but an abstract object. We can refer to concepts only by predicates used *as* predicates. Similarly, any predicate that we attach to such a subject-term as 'The concept of being a whale'—e.g. the predicate 'is subordinate to the concept of being a mammal'—does not refer to a second-level concept but to an abstract first-level one. Second-level concepts are referred to by expressions like 'Everything that . . . is red-blooded', which are not predicates in the ordinary sense at all. 'Second-level concepts, which concepts fall under, are essentially different from first-level concepts, which objects fall under'; and 'the relation of an object to a first-level concept that it falls under is different from the (admittedly similar) relation of a first-level to a second-level concept'. The main similarity between the two sorts of concepts is that they are what Frege calls 'unsaturated' (a chemical simile which Peirce also uses in connection with his rhemes). Both sorts require supplementation by something else in order to make up a complete 'thought' (i.e. what would be expressed by a sentence); though the supplementation required is different in the two cases. It might be said at this point that an 'object' also requires supplementation in order to make up a complete 'thought'; but Frege had his reasons, which we shall consider in the next section, for putting objects in a class apart.

4. *General and singular terms in* Principia Mathematica
Perhaps the most striking feature of the treatment of general
and singular terms in *Principia Mathematica* is the extent to
which that work preserves the broad standpoint of John Stuart
Mill.

In *Principia Mathematica*, as in Mill's *System*, the notion of a
'class' is essentially a derivative one. A class is the 'extension of a
propositional function', the class defined by the function f being
symbolised as '$\hat{x}(fx)$'. To be a member of the class defined by a
given propositional function is simply to be one of the objects of
which that function is true; a function being 'true of' an object if
the proposition resulting from the replacement of the variable in
the function by the name of that object is a true one. Thus if A is F,
i.e. if 'fa' is a true proposition, we may say that the function f is
true of A, and so that A is a member of the class $\hat{x}(fx)$.[1] The
boundaries of the class are fixed by its defining function; we do not
need to know what objects are members of it in order to know what
class is being referred to (Mill again); and a class may have only one
member, being then called a 'unit class', or none at all, being then
called the 'null class'. (There is only one null class; for the word
'class' is so used that if each of two functions is true of the same
objects as the other, and false of the same objects as the other, they
are said to determine one and the same class.[2] The class of featherless
bipeds is therefore identical with the class of rational animals, if all
featherless bipeds are rational animals and *vice versa*; and the class
of golden mountains is identical with the class of round squares,
since both of the functions 'x is a golden mountain' and 'x is a
round square' are true of nothing and false of everything.) A unit
class is distinguished from its one member (for example, the class
of classes identical with the null class is itself a unit class, but its
one member is not a unit class, being the null class); and the
inclusion of one class in another is distinguished from, though connected with, the membership of an object in a class (cf. the different
but connected 'imports' of universal and singular propositions in
Mill). 'The class $\hat{x}(fx)$ is included in the class $\hat{x}(gx)$' is symbolised
as '$\hat{x}(fx) \subset \hat{x}(gx)$', and 'The object A is a member of the class
$\hat{x}(fx)$' as '$a \in \hat{x}(fx)$'; and the former is defined as meaning 'If any

[1] *Principia Mathematica*, *20.02.
[2] *20.13.

object is a member of $\hat{x}(fx)$ then that object is a member of $\hat{x}(gx)$', or symbolically, '$(y):y \in \hat{x}(fx) . \supset . y \in \hat{x}(gx)$'.[1]

The dependence, in both Mill's *System* and the *Principia*, of membership in a class upon the possession of the class's 'defining characteristic' (or upon the satisfying of its defining function) throws some light upon Lord Russell's paradox about the class of all classes not members of themselves. The paradox, it will be remembered, is that when we attempt to decide whether this class itself is or is not a member of itself, we find that if it is, it follows that it is not, while if it is not, it follows that it is. As in the case of the *Liar*, the paradox seems to arise from the attempt to make a one-sided relation of 'determination' work both ways.[2] Whether or not anything is a member of a specified class is determined by whether or not it possesses the defining characteristic of the class; consequently—the one-sidedness of this relation of 'determination' being understood—whether or not anything possesses the defining characteristic of the class cannot be determined by whether or not it is a member of it, nor can whether or not it is a member of it be determined by this. When we turn to the supposed 'class of all classes not members of themselves', and ask whether or not this class is a member of itself, we find that this depends on whether or not it possesses its own defining characteristic; but this defining characteristic is 'not being a member of itself' (that is the attribute that a class must have if it is to belong to this class of classes); hence whether or not this class is a member of itself depends on whether or not it is a member of itself, which is as repugnant to the notion of class-membership as the dependence of a proposition's truth or falsehood upon its truth or falsehood is to the notions of truth and falsehood. Exactly the same difficulty arises if we ask whether or not the class of all classes which *are* members of themselves is or is not a member of itself. Such a characteristic as being, or not being, a member of itself cannot define a class any more than the characteristic of affirming or denying its own truth can define a proposition.[3]

The consequences of this solution are, however, more far-reaching than they may at first appear. To say that the characteristic of not being a member of itself cannot define a class is to say in

---

[1] *22.01.

[2] Cf. *Formal Logic*, 288–9.

[3] Cf. *Principia Mathematica*, Introduction to 1st edition, ch. 2, sect. 8.

effect that there is no such characteristic (for what sort of a characteristic would it be which could not divide the universe into the things that possess it and the things that do not?). And this seems a strange thing to say; for *is* there not such a characteristic, and does not the class of men, for example, possess it? For the class of men, surely, is not a man; that is, it does not possess its own defining characteristic of humanity (the function '*x* is a man' is not true of it); that is, it is not a member of itself—and *that* is, it is one of the classes which are not members of themselves, i.e. is a member of the class of such classes. This seems to bring us back where we were. To maintain the solution previously given, we must deny the first premise of this last argument, namely the assertion that the class of men is not a man. But how can we deny this except by maintaining that the class of men *is* a man?—and this seems absurd. The answer of *Principia Mathematica* is that even to form a false proposition the predicates 'is a man' and 'is not a man' can only be attached to subjects of a certain 'type', namely individuals; not, for example, to classes. If we attempt to attach them to classes, the result is not a truth or a falsehood, but nonsense. And it is not difficult to see why and in what sense it is nonsense. Suppose for a moment we take the sentences 'The class of men is a man' and 'The class of men is not a man' at their face-value, and accept them both as true. The only conclusion we can then draw from them is that the class of men does not exist. And neither it does—in the sense in which a thing must 'exist' in order to be a man or not to be a man. Talk about classes, according to *Principia Mathematica*, is just talk about individuals and their characteristics, couched in an alternative form. (The sense in which a thing's being a member of a certain class is 'determined by' its possession of that class's defining characteristic is a simple one—the expression 'X is a member of the class marked off by the characteristic C' is simply *defined* as a way of saying that X has C, and the error involved in trying to turn this 'determination' in the opposite direction is simply that of circular definition.) Statements which purport to be about the properties of classes, and so about the higher-level classes into which these classes fall, have a meaning if and only if they can be translated into other statements about things and their characteristics. For example, the statement 'The class of men is one-membered' (i.e. is a member of the class of unit classes), though false, is not meaningless, because we can say what it means quite easily without mentioning classes at all. It means 'There is an individual such that whatever is human is identical with that individual'.[1] But if 'class' and 'man' are used in their ordinary senses, there can be no such translation of 'The class of men is a man' or of 'The class of men is not a man' (unless, indeed, we take the latter to be not about the class of men but about the form of words 'The class of men is a man', to the effect that this form of words does not express a true proposition, in which sense it is of course true; but in this sense we cannot infer from it that the class of men is not a member of itself). The 'theory of types', thus understood—or that part of the theory of types which admits of being understood in this way—does not really contradict the contention of Mill and Keynes against Bain that the description 'not-man' applies to every subject whatsoever to which the description 'man' does not apply; for such apparent exceptions as the class of men are not 'subjects' in the sense intended —the phrase 'the class of men' does not refer to a special subject but refers to ordinary subjects in a special way.

Turning now to singular terms, in the *Principia* as in Mill these are sharply divided into two types, proper names and definite descriptions (Mill's 'connotative individual names'). Proper names as in Mill, are simply identifying labels; though Lord Russell has insisted that in our actual understanding of grammatical proper names we always or almost always use them as descriptions. We shall return to this point in the next chapter; but we may note here that modern logicians have habitually argued that it is the demonstrative pronoun rather than the grammatical proper name which answers most closely to Mill's description of a non-connotative singular concrete name. Definite descriptions, such as 'The King of England' or 'The King of France', are analysed in a rather elaborate way, of which there is a foretaste in Mill's statement that 'it may be part of the meaning of the connotative name itself, that there can exist but one individual possessing the attribute which it connotes: as for instance, "the *only* son of John Stiles".'[2] What Lord Russell says here is that such a statement as 'The King of France is bald' means that there is an individual such that (1) he (is male and) reigns over France, (2) no other individual (is male

---

[1] Cf. *Principia Mathematica*, **52.01.1.
[2] *System of Logic*, I.ii.5.

and) reigns over France, and (3) he is bald.[1] A definite description of the form 'The thing that is F' (e.g. that reigns over France) is symbolised in the *Principia* as $(\imath x)(fx)$. It should be noted that this group of symbols, like $\hat{x}(fx)$, and unlike $(x)fx$ and $(\exists x)fx$, does not represent a proposition, but may function as a subject in propositions—we may have propositions of the form $g(\imath x)(fx)$, 'The thing that is F is G' as well as of the form fa or ga.

The Russellian analysis of descriptive singular terms has a bearing on the relation between what Lord Russell calls 'propositional functions' and the ordinary 'functions' of Mathematics. A mathematician would say that 2^2 is the same function of 2 as 3^2 is of 3, and that the value of this function for the argument 2 is 4, while for the argument 3 it is 9. He might also say such and such a function of x, say x^2, has such and such a value when $x = 2$ and such and such a value when $x = 3$. Lord Russell does not describe his 'propositional functions' as functions 'of' anything; and the 'value' of a propositional function is said to be the proposition formed when the variable in it is replaced by a symbol of fixed meaning—e.g. the value of 'x is a man' when 'x' is replaced by 'Socrates' is the proposition 'Socrates is a man'. This is a little like saying that 3^2 is the value of x^2 when $x = 3$, which is not quite what a mathematician would say; and there is nothing in Lord Russell's system corresponding to what the mathematician *would* call the value of x^2 when $x = 3$, namely 9. Lord Russell is aware of these discrepancies, and contrasts his propositional functions with what he calls the 'descriptive functions' of Mathematics. The latter always refer to some object as that which stands (uniquely) in a certain relation to some other object, e.g. to the number 4 as being the square of 2. Given any relation R, 'the thing that is R to y', or more briefly 'the R of y', is symbolised in *Principia Mathematica* as $R'y$. 'The King of France' is a descriptive function in this sense too, though not one of mathematical interest; and definite descriptions usually take this form. While distinguishing descriptive from propositional functions, Lord Russell insists that the former are definable in terms of the latter, in the general manner already indicated. The phrase 'The King of France' (or 'The square of 2')

---

[1] *Principia*, Introduction to Final Edition, ch. 3; *Introduction to Mathematical Philosophy*, pp. 176–7.

4

cannot be defined on its own, but it can be 'defined in use' by saying (as in the last paragraph) that 'The King of France is Y' means 'There is something of which the following is true: that it reigns over France, etc.', where the concluding portion is not a descriptive but a propositional function.

The opposite view was taken by Frege, whose whole theory of concepts and objects grew out of an ingenious extension of the ordinary mathematical notion of a function. An ordinary functional expression such as 'The square of 2' is in Frege's sense a proper name—the proper name of what would ordinarily be called the value of the function, in this case 4. 'The morning star' is in just the same way the proper name of Venus. The same object may have innumerable proper names; for example 'The successor of 3' is another name of the number 4, and 'The evening star' of Venus. A statement of identity linking two such proper names, e.g. 'The evening star is the morning star' or 'The successor of 3 is the square of 2', is in general quite a significant statement (one the truth of which may require to be *discovered*) and not a mere truism like 'Venus is Venus' or '4 is 4'; from which it follows that although expressions like 'The evening star' and 'The morning star' name, denote or refer to the same object, they nevertheless differ in their 'sense'. Exactly the same distinction, Frege holds, may be made in the case of complete sentences. Every sentence (apart from certain exceptions to be considered in the next chapter) denotes or names one or the other of two objects which Frege calls the True and the False; but it means, or has for its sense, a 'thought', this being not a thinking but something that may be thought, i.e. a 'proposition-in-itself'. The infinitude of true propositions are so to speak so many descriptions of the True, and the infinitude of false propositions so many descriptions of the False, just as 'The square of 2', 'The successor of 3', 'The half of 8', etc. are so many descriptions of the number 4. The form 'If and only if P then Q', with 'if' understood truth-functionally, is on this view analogous to 'The evening star is the morning star'; it is true if and only if the sentences 'P' and 'Q' denote the same truth-value, but is significant only if their senses are different, just as 'The evening star is the morning star' is true if and only if 'The evening star' and 'The morning star' denote the same object, but is significant only if their senses are different (as in fact they are).

Such a phrase as 'The square of 2' denotes the number 4 by expressing (via its 'sense') a function of the number 2. It expresses the same function of 2 as 'The square of 3' does of 3, and which number it denotes depends on which number the function it expresses has for its argument. In exactly the same way, the sentence 'Socrates is wise' expresses the same function of Socrates as 'Simple Simon is wise' does of Simple Simon, and which of the two truth-values it denotes (i.e. whether it is true or false) depends on which object this function has for its argument. The only way of expressing a function separately from its argument is by some such form as 'The square of ( )', or in the special case of propositional functions, by such a form as '( ) is wise'. These latter functions are precisely what Frege means by 'concepts'. Their 'unsaturatedness' is just the incompleteness of any function considered apart from that *of* which it is or may be a function; and their difference from descriptive functions is merely that their values, when their arguments are supplied, are truth-values. Whereas the insertion of the name 'Caesar' in the blank in the ordinary functional expression 'The murderer of ( )' will cause the whole to denote an ordinary individual, namely Brutus, and its insertion in the blank in 'The wife of ( )' will cause the whole to denote another ordinary individual, namely Calpurnia, its insertion in the blank in '( ) conquered Gaul' will cause the whole to denote the True, and its insertion in the blank in '( ) conquered China' will cause the whole to denote the False. Second-level concepts are also 'functions'—and we get sentences denoting truth-values when their arguments are supplied. Thus the insertion of the predicate 'is a man' in the blank in 'Whatever ( ) is mortal' will cause the whole ('Whatever is a man is mortal') to denote the True. So, of course, will the insertion of the same predicate in 'Socrates ( )', so that this too may be regarded as a second-level concept-expression; but this second-level concept-expression is not identical with the name 'Socrates', for the name 'Socrates' already denotes an object just as the sentence 'Socrates is a man' does (though, of course, a different object—not the True, but Socrates).[1]

5. *The Elimination of abstract nouns*

An aspect of Mill's theory of naming to which we have not yet given

[1] Cf. P. T. Geach, 'Subject and Predicate', *Mind* 1950, p. 474.

much attention is his account of abstract nouns. His view of these is that these 'denote attributes' in much the same way as proper names denote things; and they denote precisely the attributes which are *co*nnoted by the corresponding general name or adjective.[1] Thus 'man' denotes individual men by connoting the attribute of humanity (i.e. not mankind, but human-ness), and this same attribute is not connoted but denoted by the word 'humanity'. A similar theory is propounded by Johnson, who says that 'orange' is the proper name of the 'adjective', i.e. attribute, of which 'the colour between red and yellow' is a definite description, exactly as 'Snowdon' is the proper name of the 'substantive', i.e. thing, of which 'the highest mountain in Wales' is a definite description.[2] Frege's theory, it will be recalled, is a little different—he regards predicative expressions, not as referring indirectly to the same entities as abstract denotative expressions refer to directly, but as referring to different entities (to concepts, while the latter refer to the associated abstract objects).

The theory of Mill and Johnson has a bearing on the medieval disputes between Realists, Conceptualists and Nominalists. These disputes were primarily about the meaning, not of abstract terms, but of common ones. 'Man' seems to refer, not to an individual thing, but to a 'kind' of thing; but does the real world include 'kinds of thing' as well as individual things? The Realists held that it does; the Nominalists held that common terms are mere words which we use to refer to individuals; and the Conceptualists, in between, held that such terms refer to something in our minds by means of which we think of individuals. As far as 'kinds of things' are concerned, and most emphatically as far as 'classes' of things are concerned, Mill is a nominalist—common terms are only part of a particular way of talking, not about classes, but about individuals. But he can only explain *how* we use common terms to talk about individuals, by taking a realist view of 'attributes'. We call different things by the same common name because they really do have common attributes, which can in their turn be named individually. Mill is particularly clear on this point in a footnote[3] in which he considers a suggestion of Herbert Spencer's that Socrates and Alcibiades are not both called men because one and the same

---

[1] *System*, I.ii.5.
[2] *Logic*, I.vi.2.
[3] To the *System of Logic*, II.iii.3.

attribute (of humanity) is possessed by them both, but because a certain attribute of one of them is *exactly like* a certain attribute of the other. Mill suggests that Spencer is confusing an 'attribute' with the particular sensations in which it is manifested to us; and if Spencer suggests that it is 'the similarity of the feelings' which leads us to apply the one name, Mill's rejoinder is that 'the attribute is precisely that similarity'. He hints at the infinite regress that besets us if we say that 'if a hundred sensations are undistinguishably alike', their resemblance ought not to be spoken of one resemblance but as 'a hundred resemblances which merely *resemble* one another'. 'The things compared are many, but the something common to them all must be conceived as one, just as the name is conceived as one, though corresponding to numerically different sensations of sound each time it is pronounced.' The latter part of this sentence is an interesting anticipation of Peirce's distinction between words as 'types' and as 'tokens'; and Mill himself uses the word 'type' a little further on, when he explains that by an attribute he does not mean a sensation but a type of sensation. A theory not unlike Spencer's has been propounded in the present century by Cook Wilson, Joseph, Stout and McTaggart and criticised in very much Mill's manner.[1]

Turning to *Principia Mathematica*, the position here seems to be much as in Mill. It is not always clear in *Principia Mathematica* whether a 'propositional function' is a group of symbols of the form 'ϕx' or what such a group of symbols means; but 'functions' in the latter sense seem to be involved in the *Principia* explanation of the use of the term 'class', as 'attributes' are involved in the corresponding explanation in Mill's *System*. The *Principia* also has a symbolism for referring directly to functions instead of merely predicating them of their arguments. (When they are thus directly spoken about, a circumflex is placed over their variable.) But there are other elements in the *Principia* which suggest a more nominalistic view.

Part of the theory of types is that neither a function nor its negation can significantly take itself as an argument, any more than a

[1] See, e.g., the debate between Joseph and Ramsey, *Universals and the 'Method of Analysis'*, Arist. Soc. Supp. Vol. VI (1926); also Broad's *Examination of McTaggart's Philosophy*, vol. 1, pp. 25-6; and for a very full study of the subject, Professor Kemp Smith's three articles on the subject in *Mind* 1927.

class can have itself as a member. 'Redness is red' and 'Redness is not red' are just as meaningless as 'The class of red things is red' and 'The class of red things is not red'. For if we can say that redness is not red, we can infer that redness does not characterise itself, and if there is such a characteristic (i.e. function) as that of not characterising itself, we can ask whether this characteristic itself characterises itself or not, and from either answer to this question we can infer the opposite answer. Up to a point, this paradox can be dealt with in the same way as the others. Whether or not the characteristic of being Y characterises X is determined in every case by whether or not X is Y; and this determination is irreversible; the paradox arises when we try to consider as a characteristic something for which the determination would have to work in both directions. But can we, as in the case of the paradox about classes, regard the 'determination' in question as simply the definition of one way of talking in terms of another? That we can, is strongly suggested in the second edition of *Principia Mathematica*, and much more than suggested in a paper of Lord Russell's on *Logical Atomism*.[1] On this view such a statement as 'Wisdom characterises Socrates', or 'That he is wise is true of Socrates' (a formulation which turns the abstract noun into something more obviously equivalent to the Russellian '$\phi\hat{x}$'), can be defined as meaning simply 'That Socrates is wise is true'; 'That he is wise has been asserted of Socrates' (i.e. 'Wisdom has been ascribed to Socrates') can be similarly defined as meaning simply 'It has been asserted that Socrates is wise'; and it is because 'Wisdom is wise', or 'That he is wise is wise' cannot be given any such restatement that it has the meaninglessness which the theory of types compels us to ascribe to it. The programme of modern nominalism has largely consisted in trying thus to reduce all obviously true statements in which the apparent subjects are abstract nouns or equivalent clauses to merely verbal variants of statements in which the subjects are individuals and the abstract nouns have been replaced by the corresponding predicative expressions.

There is perhaps a hint of something like this programme in Aristotle's statement that although substances (things), qualities, relations, places, times, etc. may all be said in a sense to 'be', this

[1] In *Contemporary British Philosophy*, 1st series (1924). See especially pp. 371–6.

can only be said of them in different senses, and yet not in totally disconnected senses, all the other senses of 'being' being derived from that in which it is asserted of 'substances'.[1] Substitute 'be something' (e.g. wise, or red) for 'be' (and indeed Aristotle's 'be' often seems to mean 'be something'), and you seem to have substantially the modern doctrine. The 'programme of nominalism' is, nevertheless, beset with difficulties. In the first place, the kind of reduction so far illustrated seems merely to eliminate one sort of abstract entity by restoring another, namely the 'proposition in itself'. It puts an end, at all events, to the ascriptive theory of believing as a means of eliminating the latter. For we cannot clear 'Plato believed that Socrates was wise' from the imputation of expressing a relation between Plato and a proposition-in-itself by saying that it merely means 'Wisdom was ascribed to Socrates by Plato', if we say at the same time that 'Wisdom was ascribed to Socrates by Plato', or 'That he was wise was believed of Socrates by Plato', is merely a way of saying 'Plato believed that Socrates was wise'. Nor is it easy to see how we can explain away the reference to objective characters in such a statement as 'Plato and Socrates had a number of characters in common'. We could say, of course, that this just means that 'Socrates and Plato were alike'; but what do we do then with 'The likenesses of Plato and Socrates were more numerous than their differences'? What, again, do we do with 'Red (i.e. redness) is a colour', or 'The colours of things are determined by their chemical constitution'? We might say for the latter 'How a thing looks depends on what it is made of' but the subject of this is still the abstract 'How a thing looks', so we might just as well say 'colour' and be done with it.

An alternative explanation which has recently been suggested for the 'meaninglessness' of such expressions as 'Redness is red' and 'Redness is not red' is that these are simply things which we 'do not want to say'. 'We may often want to say that a flower or a book is or is not red, but never that redness is or is not red. We may want to say that a soldier is or is not brave, but never that courage is not brave. We may want to say that a bit of wood is or is not triangular, but never that triangularity is or is not triangular. What could be

---

[1] The connection between Aristotle's theory of categories and the modern theory of types is noted in Professor Ryle's paper 'Categories', *Proc. Arist. Soc.* 1937–8.

the point of such locutions?' We cannot therefore regard this part of the theory of types as 'unnatural' or its prohibitions as 'real propositions'. 'In a park a notice "Do not sit on the bench" is a real prohibition, but "Do not sit on the cactus" is hardly so.'[1] Speaking for myself (when an appeal is thus made to one's likes and dislikes, for whom else can one speak?), it is true that I have generally no desire to sit on cactus, but I do want to say that redness is not red. I want to say it because (to give no other reasons) only material objects are red, and redness is not a material object, and from this 'Redness is not red' seems to follow by simple syllogism.[2] (If we are not as sure about de Morgan's syllogisms as we are about Aristotle's, it is an easy enough matter to turn it into Camestres.)[3] Perhaps the answer to this is that, whatever may be the case with me, persons whose instincts in these matters are more 'natural' than mine would not want to say 'Redness is not red'. To this I have no answer. I do not mean that it is true, but just that there is nothing that I 'want to say' about it. Or perhaps the answer is that, whatever I or even more 'natural' persons may want, we *ought* not to say 'Redness is not red'. And this, indeed, I am almost convinced is true—the paradoxes bear witness to it. But I am puzzled by the fact, and one of the main aims of the theory under consideration is to show that the theory of types presents no 'real' puzzle. Perhaps, again, it may be said, with my syllogism particularly in view, that 'Redness is not a material object' is not really about redness but about 'redness', and means ' "Redness" is not a material-object-word'. Professor Carnap calls this the translation of a statement from the 'material' to the 'formal' mode of speech; other writers call it minding one's inverted commas. 'Minding one's inverted commas' generally consists in inserting them where no one would naturally dream of doing so. There is, all the same, something to be said for doing it, as there is for most of the 'unnatural' transformations of statements in which logicians indulge, provided that it is rightly understood. What is meant by a 'material-object-word'? One which it 'makes sense' to fit into the blank in such 'sentence-frames' as

---

[1] I take these statements from a paper 'Paradoxes and Logical Types' by Professor J. J. C. Smart, discussed at the 1951 Congress of the Australasian Association of Psychology and Philosophy.

[2] Cf. H. H. Price, Arist. Soc. Supp. Vol. IX (1929), p. 111.

[3] Cf. *Formal Logic*, p. 133.

'— is red' and '— is not red'?[1] In this case, the expression can hardly be introduced in an explanation of how it is that 'Redness is not red' does not make sense. Or is a material-object-word one which refers to material objects, while redness does not refer to a material object but to something else? In that case, why can we not talk about this something else as well as the word that refers to it, and say 'Redness is not a material object'—and for that matter 'Redness is not red'—as well as 'Redness' is not a material-object-word? The translation into the 'formal mode' only helps if it means that words like 'redness' have meaning in a different way—a more indirect way, it may be—from material-object-words. But this is just the theory that we have already considered; and in the form in which we considered it, it looks as if it will not do. There may, however, prove to be more satisfactory forms of it; it is in this general direction, at all events, that most hope of progress seems to lie.

---

[1] Cf. G. Ryle, *Proc. Arist. Soc.* 1937–8, p. 193.

CHAPTER FIVE

Existential Propositions and the Existential Import of Categorical Propositions

1. *Mill's flame-breathing serpent*

In Mill's *System of Logic*[1] there is propounded a puzzle which in effect takes its rise from the following syllogism about a syllogism:

(1) Every syllogism of the form 'Any Y is Z, and any Y is X, therefore some X is Z', with two true premisses, has a true conclusion; and

(2) The syllogism 'A dragon breathes flame, and a dragon is a serpent, therefore some serpent breathes flame', is a syllogism of the form 'Any Y is Z, and any Y is X, therefore some X is Z', with two true premisses;

Therefore (3) the syllogism 'A dragon breathes flame, and a dragon is a serpent, therefore some serpent breathes flame', has a true conclusion—that is, some serpent really does breathe flame.

This syllogism (that is, the outer one) is in Barbara (or, if we treat singulars as particulars, in Darii); one can hardly question its validity. Of its premisses, the major simply affirms the validity of syllogisms in the mood Darapti. The minor asserts that the syllogism about dragons is a syllogism in this mood, as it plainly is, with two true premisses, the truth of the premisses being guaranteed by the fact that 'a dragon' is *defined* as 'a flame-breathing serpent'. Yet the conclusion, so far as we know, is false. This fact leads Mill in effect to propound an opponent syllogism in Figure 2, namely

(1) Every syllogism of the form 'Any Y is Z, etc.', with two true premisses, has a true conclusion;

But (not-3) the syllogism 'A dragon breathes flame, etc.' has not a true conclusion;

[1] I.viii.5.

Therefore (not-2) the syllogism 'A dragon breathes flame, etc.' is not a syllogism of the form 'Any X is Y, etc.' with two true premisses —that is, either the syllogism about dragons has not two true premisses, or it is not of the form in question. Mill's view is that which of these alternatives we must take depends on how we interpret the premisses. The conclusion plainly means 'Some really existing serpent is a really existing flame-breather', and if the premisses mean respectively 'A dragon is a really existing flame-breather' and 'A dragon is a really existing serpent', then the syllogism is indeed in Darapti, but (so Mill argues) its premisses are false, for the definition of 'dragon' does not guarantee their truth in *this* sense. A definition is not a statement about really existing things but one about the meaning of words, so that it guarantees the truth of the premisses only if they are interpreted as equivalent respectively to '*Dragon* is a word meaning a thing which breathes flame' and '*Dragon* is a word meaning a serpent'; but when they are thus interpreted, the syllogism is not in Darapti or in any other valid form, for the only conclusion that follows in Darapti is 'Some word which means a serpent is a word which means a thing breathing flame'. Or, Mill adds, the premisses might mean 'The *idea* of a dragon is an idea of a thing which breathes flame' and 'The idea of a dragon is an idea of a serpent'; from which all that follows in Darapti is that some idea of a serpent is an idea of a thing which breathes flame.

Substantially the same solution is given by some Neo-scholastic writers, such as Maritain, who argue that the trouble with such syllogisms is that the terms have different 'suppositions' in the premisses and the conclusion. In the conclusion, the word 'serpent' stands for (*supponit pro*) really existing things which are serpents; in its premiss it stands for itself as a word—'A dragon is a serpent', in the sense in which it is true, means that one part of what the word 'dragon' means is what the word 'serpent' means—or else for the corresponding idea.

But what *does* the word 'dragon' mean? It means, surely, a really existing thing; that is, it is only to really existing things that we would apply it, if we applied it at all. It is not the name of a word, or of an idea. 'Dragons do not exist' does not mean 'There is no such word as *dragon*', nor does it mean 'There is no such idea as the idea of a dragon'; it means 'There is no such *thing* as a dragon'.

Similarly, 'A dragon would frighten me if I saw one' does not mean 'The word *dragon* would frighten me if I saw it', nor does it mean 'The idea of a dragon would frighten me if I saw it'. (No one, in fact, has argued more powerfully or more cogently than Mill himself against the theory that names are not used to stand for things themselves but only for our ideas of things.)[1] 'A dragon breathes flame' therefore does mean 'Any dragon there may be is a really existing thing which breathes flame'; and furthermore, '*Dragon* is a word which means a thing which breathes flame' means '*Dragon* is a word which we would apply only to really existing things which breathe flame'. No proposition about what words mean is about words alone, for such a proposition tells us what attributes a 'really existing thing' must have if we are to apply the word to it; and the proposition 'Any dragon there may be is a (really existing) thing which breathes flame' is as much guaranteed by our definition as the other. Moreover, it is quite easy to drop the word 'Dragon' altogether, and replace it by what we have decided to mean by it, and Mill's syllogism will remain as puzzling as ever. For it will then become

> Any flame-breathing serpent there may be is a (really existing) thing which breathes flame,
> And any flame-breathing serpent there may be is a (really existing) serpent,
> Therefore some serpent breathes flame.[2]

What, then, shall we put in the place of this solution? One possibility is to accept the conclusion of our original first-figure syllogism about this syllogism, and revise our opinion as to the non-existence of flame-breathing serpents. They do not exist, indeed, in the ordinary world around us (which contains the word 'Dragon', and our ideas of dragons, but no dragons); but perhaps there is some other world, just as real as the familiar one, in which they do exist. This is a conclusion which many philosophers have arrived at, in any case, by a shorter route. 'Dragons do not exist', it may be argued, is the sort of statement which must be either false or

---

[1] *System of Logic*, I.ii.1, I.v.1. Cf. Russell, *Introduction to Mathematical Philosophy*, pp. 169–70.

[2] Cf. Keynes, *Formal Logic*, 4th ed., §346; Venn, *Symbolic Logic*, 2nd ed., p. 153, n. 1.

meaningless. For either there is some real thing which the word 'dragon' means, or there is not. But if there is, the statement that dragons do not exist is false; and if there is not, the word 'dragon' is meaningless, and the statement 'Dragons do not exist' therefore meaningless also. This is the argument which Professor Quine[1] calls 'Plato's beard', the conclusion which it suggests being the sort of conclusion which the maxim called 'Ockham's Razor'—'entities are not to be multiplied beyond necessity' (*entia non sunt multiplicanda praeter necessitatem*)—instructs us to attempt to avoid. But is there not a *necessitas* here which makes the maxim inapplicable? The answer to this is implicit in what has been said in an earlier chapter about the meaning of general terms; but to see what that answer is, we must return to our syllogism.

A way of escape which we have yet to consider is the construction of the *other* opponent syllogism to the first-figure one from which we began—the one which falls into Figure 3. This syllogism will run

(Not-3) The syllogism 'A dragon breathes flame, etc.' has not a true conclusion;

But (2) the syllogism 'A dragon breathes flame, etc.' is a syllogism of the form 'Any Y is Z, etc.' with two true premisses;

Therefore (not-1) not every syllogism of the form 'Any Y is Z, etc.', with two true premisses, has a true conclusion.

Darapti, in other words, is not a valid inferential form. What, then, is wrong with it? It breaks none of the traditional syllogistic rules. Moreover, the very syllogism which we have just used to demonstrate its invalidity is itself in the mood in question.[2]

Putting this last point on one side for a moment, we may say that what is wrong with the syllogism about dragons is obviously that its conclusion implies the existence of flame-breathing serpents, while

---

[1] In his article 'On What There Is' in the *Review of Metaphysics*, Sept. 1948; reproduced in Arist. Soc. Supp. Vol. XXV (1951).

[2] [In fact, if a syllogism has a conclusion saying that not all instances of the mood there employed are valid, this conclusion must itself be true if the premisses are true. Clearly this is so if the syllogism is valid; and if it is invalid, then again its conclusion is true. Eds.]

its premisses do not imply the existence of either serpents or flame-breathers, let alone beings which are both. For we may dispose of 'Plato's beard' simply by saying that propositions beginning 'Any Y . . .' or 'Any Y there may be . . .' do *not* imply that anything is in fact a Y. Such propositions do, indeed, refer to 'really existing things', but they do not say of any such thing that it is in fact a Y; what they say of really existing things is simply that *if* any of them is a Y it is Z'. It is the word 'any' that imports this 'hypothetical-ness' into such a proposition; and it is because the indefinite article in 'A dragon breathes flame' has the force of 'Any' rather than of 'Some' that these considerations apply to it. This may be made plain by considering a syllogism in which the indefinite article is used in the other sense—say the syllogism

A dragon breathes flame,
And a dragon molested the Thebans yesterday,
Therefore something that molested the Thebans yesterday breathes flame.

In the second premiss here 'A dragon' means 'Some dragon', so that the syllogism is not in Darapti but in Datisi; and if we are right in supposing that there are no dragons, this premiss will be false, so there would be nothing surprising in the conclusion's being false also. This also explains why the syllogism by which we have shown the invalidity of the form 'Any Y is Z, etc.' is not itself affected. We may classify it as being in Darapti, but its premisses do not begin with 'Any Y . . .', for they are not genuine universals but singulars. (They begin 'The syllogism, etc.'.) The same observation applies to the syllogism with the premisses '*Dragon* is a word meaning a flame-breather' and '*Dragon* is a word meaning a serpent', which Mill substitutes for his original one.

This contention as to the meaning of the form 'Any Y is Z' is in accordance with Russell's view that what it expresses is a 'formal implication'. It is equally in accordance with the view of Mill himself that general propositions are to be read 'in connotation'. What the proposition 'Any dragon breathes flame' is about, in the sense in which a proposition's being about a thing implies that that thing exists, is not dragons but the properties of breathing flame and being a serpent which the word 'dragon' connotes. It asserts that wherever these two properties are found in conjunction (though that may be nowhere), the property of breathing flame will be found; and this can hardly be questioned.

2. *Existential propositions in Bretano*

This consequence of Mill's interpretation of universal propositions is one which Mill himself failed to see, though one of his correspondents, namely Brentano, did his best to make him aware of it. Mill held that affirmative propositions always imply that their subject-terms exist except when they are merely verbal (and then, of course, they imply the existence of the corresponding words). Brentano's views on the subject are developed in a chapter of his *Psychology*[1] in which he is arguing that the passing of a judgement and the entertaining of an idea are two fundamentally different states of mind. One of the opposing theories which he had to consider was the theory that the passing of a judgement is merely the formation (by 'association of ideas') of a complex conception. This view had been held by J. S. Mill's father, James Mill, and Mill (the younger) agreed with Brentano in opposing it. 'We may,' Mill argues in his *Logic*,[2] 'put two ideas together without any act of belief; as when we merely imagine something, such as a golden mountain; or when we actually disbelieve: for in order even to disbelieve that Mahomet was an apostle of God, we must put the idea of Mahomet and that of an apostle of God together.' Brentano thought this argument conclusive, but supplements it with another. We may, he says, pass judgements which do not involve two 'ideas' at all, but only one, for example the judgement that A is, or that A is not. To this, of course, it can be replied that there is another idea beside that of A involved in such judgements, namely the idea of existence. Brentano's answer is that there is no such idea. To prove this, he sets out to undermine the distinction made in the traditional logic between the 'existential' and the 'copulative' uses of the word 'is' (between 'is' *secundi* and 'is' *tertii adjecti*). This point was important to his argument because he could count upon his opponents to agree that when 'is' is used as a copula it does not represent a distinct 'idea' but only the bringing together of the 'ideas' represented by the subject and the predicate. His manner of breaking down the distinction is to say that a proposition in which 'is' is employed as a

[1] Bk. II, ch. 7.
[2] I.v.I.

copula is always equivalent to one in which it is employed existentially. For 'Every X is Y' simply means 'X-without-Y does not exist'; 'No X is Y' means 'X-with-Y does not exist'; 'Some X is Y' means 'X-with-Y exists'; and 'Some X is not Y' means 'X-without-Y exists'. Since 'exists' in these forms simply replaces the copula of the traditional forms, it can represent no distinct idea, and must represent the act of the mind accepting or rejecting the complex ideas 'X-with-Y' or 'X-without-Y' as the case may be. And since it plainly has the same sense when what is said to exist or not to exist is the simple X or A, in this case also it cannot represent a distinct idea before the mind, but only the mind's act of accepting or rejecting.

Into this fundamentally psychological argument, Brentano inserts a logical digression. This view of the meaning of universal and particular propositions, he argues, necessitates a complete revision of the traditional rules of the syllogism. For it means that all ordinary universal propositions are negative (denying the existence either of X-with-Y or of X-without-Y) and all particulars affirmative (affirming the existence of one or the other of these), so that all syllogisms in which both premisses are universal will have two negative premisses. Every syllogism, moreover, will contain four terms, two of them being one another's contradictories. Barbara, for example, will have the form

$$Y\text{-and-not-}Z? - No!$$
$$X\text{-and-not-}Y? - No!$$
$$\text{Hence: } X\text{-and-not-}Z? - No!$$

Here the terms are X, Y, not-Y and not-Z. (The question-mark indicates the bare entertainment of the complex idea which precedes it, while the 'Yes!' and 'No!' indicate the supervening acceptance or rejection.) Darii will appear as

$$Y\text{-and-not-}Z? - No!$$
$$X\text{-and-}Y? \quad - Yes!$$
$$\text{Hence: } X\text{-and-}Z? \quad - Yes!$$

Here the terms are X, Y, Z and not-Z. And similarly with the rest. All syllogisms, Brentano goes on, are governed by the rules that if the conclusion is 'negative', both the premisses will share its quality

and contain one of its terms (see Barbara above), while if the conclusion is 'affirmative' one of the premisses will share its quality and
contain one of its terms, while the other will be opposed in quality
and contain the contradictory of the other term (see Darii above).
A consequence of the last rule is that a particular, or as Brentano
calls it an 'affirmative', conclusion must have at least one particular
premiss, thus ruling out the moods Darapti, Felapton, Bramantip
and Fesapo, and the subaltern moods. The invalidity of such a mood
as Darapti is evident if we express it in the manner which Brentano's
theory suggests:

> Dragon and not fire-breathing? — No!
> Dragon and not serpent? — No!
> Hence: Serpent and fire-breathing? — Yes!

Immediate inferences by subalternation and conversion *per accidens*
are also ruled out. (The syllogistic moods invalidated are, it will be
noted, the ones whose names end with a 'p', i.e. those which involve
conversion *per accidens* in their reduction.) We cannot, for example,
pass from

> Dragon and not serpent? — No!
> (i.e. 'Any dragon is a serpent') to
> Dragon and serpent? — Yes!
> ('Some dragon is a serpent'), or to
> Serpent and dragon? — Yes!
> ('Some serpent is a dragon');

for no assent is given to 'Dragon', i.e. the existence of dragons is not
affirmed, in the premiss, but it is affirmed in both conclusions. The
irritation which Brentano's manner of expressing these results was
calculated to produce in conservative logicians duly appeared,
though the results were not in fact as novel as he imagined. In fact,
long ago Duns Scotus, for example, was quite well aware that
'syllogisms' with two negative premisses may be valid if a term is
finite sumptus in one premiss and *infinite sumptus* in the other.

On the more fundamental issue of the equivalence of the existential and the copulative 'is', Mill (as well as others) was unconvinced.
In his *Logic* he complains, even, that the distinction had not been
properly noticed by writers before his father.[1] This is certainly, as

[1] *System of Logic*, I.iv.I.

Brentano points out, quite unhistorical. Not that Brentano, on his side, was the first to deny that existence is a genuine predicate. The point had been very emphatically made by Hume. 'The idea of existence', he says in his *Treatise*,[1] 'is the very same with the idea of what we conceive to be existent. To reflect on any thing simply, and to reflect on it as existent, are nothing different from each other . . . Any idea we please to form is the idea of a being; and the idea of a being is any idea we please to form.' And Hume drew from this the conclusion that ' 'tis far from being true, that in every judgment which we form we unite two different ideas; since in that proposition, *God is*, or indeed any other which regards existence, the idea of existence is no distinct idea which we unite with the idea of the object and which is capable of forming a compound idea by the union'.[2] He also argued that 'as 'tis certain there is a great difference betwixt the simple conception of the existence of an object and the belief of it, and as this difference lies not in the parts or composition of the idea which we conceive, it follows that it must lie in the *manner* in which we conceive it'.[3] This is close to Brentano's argument from the same premisses to the conclusion that judgement must be a mental act different in kind from mere conception, though Hume's conclusion does not reach quite as far as that.[4] Again, in dealing with the ontological proof of the existence of God—the argument that since God by definition has all perfections, and existence is a perfection, He must have that one too—Gassendi had argued that existence is not a 'perfection' but rather something presupposed in anything's having perfections,[5] and Kant argued in the same connection and in the same way that existence is not a predicate.[6] In the time of Mill and Brentano, Alexander Bain sought to eliminate the conception of existence in a somewhat different way. A proposition of the form 'X exists', Bain held, is only intelligible if the X in question is complex, i.e. if what we

[1] I.ii.6.

[2] I.iii.7, footnote.

[3] Ibid., text.

[4] Bretano has arguments against Hume's view too; but we need not concern ourselves with them.

[5] *The Philosophical Works of Descartes* (Haldane & Ross), vol. 2, p. 185. See, on this passage, W. Kneale, *Is Existence a Predicate?*, Arist. Soc. Supp. Vol .XV (1936).

[6] *Critique of Pure Reason*, Transcendental Dialectic, II.iii.5.

really have is 'A B exists', and this is just a manner of saying 'Some A is B'. This view stands Brentano on his head. But Mill, in the face of this chorus, kept to the old paths. His answer to Bain is interesting. At this point, he says in effect, his disciple is deserting him, to take up a position curiously reminiscent of the logical fantasies of a Hegel. For 'Hegel, finding that Being is an abstraction reached by thinking away all particular attributes, arrived at the self-contradictory proposition, on which he founded all his philosophy, that Being is the same as nothing'. But the true conclusion to be drawn is that 'it is the name of Something, taken in the most comprehensive sense of the word'.[1]

In this criticism of Bain there is the germ of an answer to Brentano also, though Mill does not formulate this answer. In stating his view that an existential judgement may have an uncompounded subject, Brentano does not give examples, but presents us with the formulae 'A is' and 'A is not'. Just what sort of term does this 'A' stand for? Probably a general term of some sort—we might say 'Lions exist', for example, and 'Unicorns do not exist'. But even the simplest general terms, Mill might have pointed out, have a double aspect. They have connotation and they have (or may have) denotation. They direct us both to some description that things may answer to, and to the things that may answer to this description. And what 'A exists' really tells us is that at least one of these things does answer to the description connoted by A. It means, in short, 'Something is A'.

That existence can only be intelligibly predicated of a subject that is descriptive in character, and that the real predicate in such assertions is not existence but the description connoted by the apparent subject, has been asserted in our own century by Lord Russell.[2] On this view we may intelligibly say such things as 'Lions exist', 'Unicorns do not exist', 'The King of England exists', 'The King of France does not exist'; but '*This* exists' and 'This does not exist' alike mean nothing. (The same would have to be said, I think, of 'Everything exists', 'Something exists' and 'Nothing exists', but here Lord Russell does not speak with one voice.) We can say 'Lions

---

[1] *System of Logic*, I.v.5, footnote.
[2] See, in particular, the *Introduction to Mathematical Philosophy*, ch. 16. See also G. E. Moore's paper, 'The Conception of Reality' (*Proc. Arist. Soc.* 1917–18; *Philosophical Studies*, VI).

exist' because it means 'Something is a lion'; 'Unicorns do not exist', because it means 'Nothing is a unicorn'; 'The King of England exists', because it means 'Something reigns over England, and nothing reigns over England beside it'. (Allied to this is Frege's view that existence is not a property of 'objects' but of 'concepts',[1] or more accurately that in 'An X exists' or 'Something is an X', what is asserted is that the concept signified by 'X' falls under the second-level concept signified by 'Something is a —'.) Thus Lord Russell holds with Bain and Mill against Brentano that assertions and denials of existence have a distinct subject and predicate, i.e. that affirmation and denial are not simple relations of the mind to a single (simple or complex) object—we always affirm or deny one thing of another. He agrees, on the other hand, with Bain and Brentano that in assertions and denials of existence, existence is not the real predicate, and like Bain he reduces the existential 'is' to the copulative. With Mill and Brentano, as against Bain, he holds that 'X exists' may be a genuine affirmation when the term X is non-compound, so long as it is descriptive; for although we cannot get 'Some A is B' out of 'X exists' if there is no A and B into which X may be analysed, we can predicate X of the indefinite 'Something'. And this is like Mill, with his equation of 'being' with 'Something', though this very equation, in Lord Russell's eyes, turns it from a predicate into a subject. On the subject of the syllogism, Lord Russell is substantially in agreement with Brentano. For, as we have already seen, he takes 'Every X is Y' to mean 'If anything is X it is Y', and this in turn to mean 'Nothing is in fact X without being Y', and similarly with the others; and from these interpretations the consequences to which Brentano drew attention do follow. They were, in fact, being drawn by symbolic logicians at about the time when Brentano was writing; and also one or two others of a still more paradoxical character.

3. *Existential propositions in symbolic logic*

Symbolic logic having begun as an attempt to represent propositional forms as algebraic equations, one of its earliest problems was that of finding such a representation for 'Every X is Y'. The difficulty here lies in the fact that whereas the sign of equality is convertible—if $x = y$ then $y = x$—the relation between X and Y

[1] *The Foundations of Arithmetic*, p. 53.

in 'Every X is Y' is not. '$x = y$', therefore, will not do—it represents, rather, the compound 'Every X is Y and every Y is X'. This is one of the problems which occupied Leibniz in his early experimenting with the quasi-arithmetical representation of logical forms and processes, and he managed to hit upon most of the solutions which were later worked out by the symbolists of the nineteenth century. He suggested, for example, that 'Every A is B' might be symbolised as 'A = YB', where the symbol Y means, roughly, 'some sort of'.[1] Boole used the symbol 'v' in a similar sense, regularly representing 'Every X is Y' as '$x = vy$' ('The Xs coincide with some unspecified portion of the Ys'), 'No X is Y' as '$x = v(1 - y)$', 'Some X is Y' as '$vx = vy$' ,and 'Some X is not Y' as '$vx = v(1 - y)$' (it being understood that the vs on the different sides of the equality sign cannot be cancelled out). Leibniz extended his variant of this notation to particulars in a similar manner.[2] Leibniz observed, however, that in the case of the universals, his indefinite symbol 'Y' could easily be eliminated. For by employing the law of tautology, BB = B, we may change the form 'A = YB' into 'A = YBB', and since, *ex hypothesi*, 'A = YB', we may here replace YB by A, obtaining 'A = AB'.[3] That is 'Every A is B' may be represented by the assertion that the As coincide with the things that are both As and Bs. (Every man is mortal, for example, if and only if the class of men coincides with the class of mortal men.) Jevons introduced the same modification of the symbolism of Boole. Leibniz saw that there is another representation to which this one is equivalent. For if $x = xy$, $x - xy = 0$, i.e. $x(1 - y) = 0$. That is, if the Xs coincide with the things that are both Xs and Ys, then the Xs that are not also Ys are non-existent. This suggests the use of the forms '$xy = 0$' ('Nothing is both X and Y') for 'No X is Y'; '$x(1 - y) = 0$' ('Nothing is at once X and not-Y') for 'Every X is Y'; '$xy \neq 0$' or '$xy > 0$' ('Something is both X and Y') for 'Some X is Y'; and '$x(1 - y) \neq 0$' or '$x(1 - y) > 0$' ('Something is at once X and not Y') for 'Some X is not Y'. The first two forms were sometimes used for the universals by Boole, and were strongly favoured by Venn, who also employed the assertions of inequality for particulars. Leibniz used all four forms, but

[1] Couturat, *La Logique de Leibniz*, p. 345.
[2] Ibid., p. 328.
[3] Ibid., p. 346, n. 1.

was unhappy about them because he saw, as Brentano did later, that one could not justify such inferences as subalternation if these representations were used.[1]

Another equation that follows algebraically from '$x = xy$' is $xy + (1 - x) = 1$, which we may read 'What is either both X and Y, or not X, is everything', or 'Everything that is, is either both X and Y, or not X at all'. If we use 'either' non-exclusively, we may replace this by 'Everything is either Y or not X'.[2] Symbols with this meaning were favoured, among the modern symbolists, by Mitchell and Johnson; and although they did not occur to Leibniz, something approaching them did. (He saw that if every X is Y, then the Ys coincide with the things that are either X or Y.[3] Normally these form a larger class than the Ys, but they will not if there are no Xs but those which are Ys.) Leibniz also anticipated Peirce's representation of 'Every X is Y' as '$x < y$', i.e. '$x \leqslant y$'. The form Leibniz used was '$x \geqslant y$', this inversion being due to his taking the terms in comprehension rather than in extension.[4] His '$x \geqslant y$', or 'X is at least as great as Y', does not mean 'The X's include all the Y's, and perhaps other things too' (which is not equivalent to 'Every X is Y' but to 'Every Y is X'), but rather 'Being an X involves being a Y, and perhaps involves more than that'.

Most of these, and some others, are included in a list of possible interpretations of the universal and particular forms which de Morgan made out in 1850[5] (after the appearance of Boole's first work, but before the work of Jevons, Peirce, Mitchell or Venn, and independently of Leibniz). De Morgan says that the distinction between universal and particular may be replaced by (1) that of affirmative and negative, 'Every X is Y' affirming and 'Some X is not Y' denying that the Ys and the non-Xs between them fill the universe (the interpretation favoured by Mitchell); or by (2) that of

---

[1] Ibid., pp. 350–1.

[2] For since 'y' = 'Either both x and y, or y but not x', 'y or not x' = 'either both x and y, or y but not x, or not x'. But here the middle alternative 'y but not x' is redundant, this possibility being already allowed by 'not-x'. Hence 'either y or not-x' = 'either both x and y, or not x'. This reasoning fails if 'either' is interpreted exclusively, because then we cannot join alternatives of which one 'covers' another.

[3] Couturat, p. 363.

[4] Ibid., p. 335.

[5] *Transactions of the Cambridge Philosophical Society*, vol. 9, pt. 18, pp. 1–2.

non-existent and existent, 'Every X is Y' asserting the non-existence and 'Some X is not Y' the existence of what is X-but-not-Y (Venn's interpretation); or by (3) that of necessary and not-necessary; or by (4) that of conjunctive and disjunctive, 'Every X is Y' asserting that X_1 is Y *and* X_2 is Y, etc., and 'Some X is not Y' that *either* X_1 is not Y *or* X_2 is not Y, etc. His 5th, 7th and 8th interpretations we may ignore, but his 6th is Peirce's, the replacement of universal and particulars by 'conclusive' and 'inconclusive'. 'Certain X's, determinable or indeterminable, are proposed: are they Ys or not? The universal is conclusive on this point, the particular inconclusive.'

The forms with which we are principally concerned at this point are those favoured by Venn. To illustrate his interpretation of A, E, I and O propositions, Venn introduced a certain form of diagram. The representation of all four forms involved the use of a pair of interlaced circles:

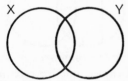

This as it stands, however, does not represent any proposition. It does not, in particular, like the corresponding Eulerian diagram, represent the assertion that Some X is Y, some X is not Y, and some Y is not X. It merely divides the universe into four parts—the part outside the diagram, which will contain anything there may be which is neither X nor Y; the part where the circles overlap, which will contain anything there may be which is both X and Y; and the other two parts, which will contain respectively anything which is X but Y and anything which is Y but not X. And the A, E, I and O forms are taken as asserting or denying that one or other of these compartments is empty. If the emptiness of a compartment is shown by shading it in, 'Every X is Y', or 'Nothing is X without being Y', will appear as

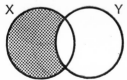

and 'No X is Y' ('Nothing is both X and Y') as

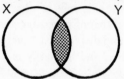

If the fact that a compartment is occupied is indicated by drawing a line across it, 'Some X is Y' will appear as

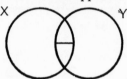

and 'Some X is not Y' as

   The representation of the premisses of syllogisms involves the use of three interlaced circles, one for each term. Taking Barbara, we begin by representing 'Every Y is Z' thus:

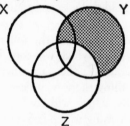

To this we add the representation of 'Every X is Y', making the whole appear as

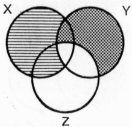

It will be noticed that among the portions now shaded is the part of the X circle which lies outside the Z zone. In other words, we have in effect asserted by this shading that nothing is at once X and not Z, i.e. that every X is Z—the syllogistic conclusion. If we are to explain in words how this has happened, we must say something like this: In representing 'Every Y is Z' we have really shaded out *two* compartments—that for 'Y but not Z, and not X either', and that for 'Y and not Z, but X'. That is, we have equated 'Every Y is Z' with the conjunction 'Nothing is at once X, Y and not-Z, and nothing is at once not-X, Y and not-Z'. The shading for 'Every X is Y' similarly equates that with 'Nothing is at once X, Z and not-Y, and nothing is at once X, not-Y and not-Z'. The total shading therefore represents the conjunction 'Nothing is at once X, Y and not-Z; nothing is at once not-X, Y and not-Z; nothing is at once X, Z and not-Y; and nothing is at once X, not-Y and not-Z'. When we discover the syllogistic conclusion, what we do in effect is to attend to the first and last components of this, i.e. to the conjunction 'Nothing is at once X, Y and not-Z; and nothing is at once X, not-Y and not-Z', and observe that what this amounts to is 'Nothing is at once X and not-Z'. This, it may be recalled, is just the sort of procedure we employed in Part I to show how syllogistic reasoning may be reduced to the form 'P and Q and R and S: therefore P and Q'. Other inferences are, of course, involved in the actual process of reduction; and these, when we inspect them, turn out to be rather like dilemmas. In particular, the concluding inference from 'Nothing is at once X, Y and not-Z, and nothing is at once X, not-Y and not-Z' to 'Nothing is at once X and not-Z', can be transformed without much difficulty into

What is both X and not-Z is not-Y,
And what is both X and not-Z is not not-Y,
Therefore nothing is both X and not-Z,

the resemblance of which to 'If P then Q, and if P then not Q, therefore not P' is obvious.

The representation of syllogisms with particular premisses is less elegant, and involves complications with which we need not here trouble ourselves. The main point to be noted is that it is impossible to validate the forms Darapti, Felapton, Bramantip and Fesapo if the above representation of A, E, I and O propositions is employed;

and in general the consequences of this representation are of the sort noted by Brentano and Leibniz. The classical treatment of this subject is that given in Keynes.[1] A point which Keynes emphasises —and it is still not always appreciated by his critics—is that what is involved here is simply a question of interpretation. If we take the form A to mean 'Nothing is X without being Y', E to mean 'Nothing is both X and Y', I to mean 'Something is both X and Y', and O to mean 'Something is X without being Y', it can hardly be questioned that their implications are as Leibniz, Brentano and Venn describe them. But we are under no compulsion to assign these meanings to these forms. We are quite entitled, if we wish, to use the form 'Every X is Y' to mean, not simply 'Nothing is X without being Y', but the compound 'Nothing is X without being Y, but something is X', and then 'Some X is Y', in the sense of 'Something is both X and Y', *will* be implied by it. Or we may, if we wish, remove the definite implication of the subject's existence from 'Some X is Y' by interpreting it, not as 'Something is both X and Y', but as 'Either something is both X and Y, or nothing is X', i.e. as 'If anything is X, then some of it is Y'.[2]

Keynes examines exhaustively the implications of the four forms in these various interpretations. His most important results are these.

(1) A and O, and E and I, will be pairs of contradictories if and only if either universals and particulars, or affirmatives and negatives, are interpreted differently as regards the implication of the subject's existence. If all four forms are taken to imply the existence of their subject, then A and O may both be false (they will be if their subjects are non-existent), and similarly with E and I. If, on the other hand, none of the forms are taken to affirm the existence of their subjects, then A and O may both be true, and so may E and I. (For example, if 'No mermaid wears spectacles' is taken to mean 'Nothing is a bespectacled mermaid' and 'Some mermaid wears spectacles' to mean 'Either something is a bespectacled mermaid, or there are no mermaids at all', both of these are true.)

(2) If, as in Brentano and Venn, the two particulars, but not the two universals, are taken to imply the existence of their subjects, then the universals will not imply the corresponding particulars, nor will they themselves be contraries. Take the notice 'All

---

[1] *Formal Logic*, 4th ed., pt. II, ch. 8.
[2] Cf. Johnson, *Logic*, I.ix.3.

trespassers on this property will be prosecuted' (a case discussed by Bradley). If nobody in fact trespassed on the property in question, we would hardly regard this as making the notice false; but it would make it true that no trespassers on this property would be prosecuted, so that in this case 'All X is Y' and 'No X is Y' would be true together.

(3) If we interpret affirmatives, but not negatives, as implying the existence of their subjects, all the traditional rules of opposition, conversion and syllogism will hold, but the obversion of negatives to affirmatives will not be valid.[1] (For example, if 'No dragon is a horse' does not imply that there are dragons, but 'Every dragon is a non-horse' does, we cannot infer the latter from the former.) There are indications, as we have seen, that Aristotle favoured this solution, and accepted its consequences.

(4) If both affirmative forms imply the existence of their subjects, then although 'Every horse is an animal' implies 'Some horse is an animal', it does not imply 'Every blue horse is an animal'; for 'Every blue horse is an animal', on this interpretation, implies the existence of blue horses, while 'Every horse is an animal' only implies the existence of horses. On the other hand, on the Brentano-Venn interpretation, while 'Every horse is an animal' does not imply 'Some horse is an animal' (since it does not imply that there are any horses), it does imply 'Every blue horse is an animal' (for 'Nothing is a horse without being an animal' implies 'Nothing is a blue horse without being an animal'). Quite generally it is only on the Brentano-Venn interpretation that inferences involving complex terms can be handled with any ease and elegance; that is why it has generally found favour among symbolic logicians.

(5) To these points we may add another, namely that even where their subjects and predicates are the same, only propositions which do not imply the existence of their subjects can be regarded as logical laws. For example, logic does not guarantee the truth of the proposition 'Every flame-breathing serpent is a flame-breathing serpent' if this is interpreted as informing us that there are flame-breathing serpents. (This has a bearing, of course, on Mill's syllogism.)

[1] Keynes does not consider this interpretation as fully as he does some of the others, but mentions the point about obversion on p. 226, n. 1, and Johnson includes it in the set of schemes considered in his *Logic*, pt. I, p. 138.

Keynes also discusses the question as to which interpretations of the four forms are closest to ordinary usage, while properly insisting that this is not a point of decisive logical importance. His conclusion as regards the universal affirmative form is that sometimes we use it in such a way that we would regard such a proposition as false if its subject were non-existent, and sometimes we do not; 'All trespassers on this property will be prosecuted' being an instance of the latter use. Here he is surely right, but there are one or two things to be added to what he says. We do, I think, normally use 'All trespassers on this property will be prosecuted' in such a way that its truth would be *consistent* with the non-existence of such trespassers; but not in such a way that it would *follow* from that. But if it just means 'Nothing is in fact a trespasser-on-this-property-that-will-not-be-prosecuted', it does follow from 'Nothing is in fact a trespasser on this property'. (So, of course, does 'Nothing is a trespasser-on-this-property that *will* be prosecuted'.) What we normally take it to mean is, I think, 'Nothing *could* be a trespasser-on-this-property-that-will-not-be prosecuted', and this is different from both of Keynes's main interpretations of the A form. He does, however, discuss forms of this sort, and what he says about them we shall consider at a later point.[1]

The implication of 'Every X is Y' by 'Nothing is X', when the former is taken to mean 'Nothing is X without being Y', is something we have already encountered as one of the paradoxes associated with Lord Russell's 'formal' implication. It is sometimes expressed in the form 'The null class is included in every class'; and though it may seem strange to say that the class of mermaids, because it is null, is included in the class of dressing-tables, this is undoubtedly true if all it means is that nothing at the same time belongs to the class of mermaids and does not belong to the class of dressing-tables. And we do occasionally use the A form in such a way that this sort of implication is legitimate; though usually it is in a half-jesting manner. Suppose a land-owner puts up a notice saying that all trespassers on his property will be prosecuted, though he has in fact no intention of prosecuting. His notice, we would then normally say, expresses a falsehood, and we would not regard it as any the less of a falsehood if nobody in fact ever did trespass on the property. Still, the landlord might say under these circumstances,

[1] Pt. v, ch. 1, §4.

though not very seriously, 'Well, I'm prosecuting all the trespassers there are'.

Something must also be said of an interpretation of the traditional four forms which Keynes nowhere directly considers, but which is mentioned by Johnson,[1] and which has received considerable attention during the past few years. This is the view that what we normally intend to convey by 'Every X is Y' is something which, when nothing is X, is neither true nor false but meaningless. We may best understand this point of view by considering propositions as giving the sense of affirmative or negative answers to questions. Aristotle, it will be remembered, argued that there are questions to which such answers cannot be given, because two or more distinct questions are asked as if they were one. Many later writers, such as Whately, have put under this 'Fallacy of Many Questions' cases in which the very asking of a question presupposes an affirmative answer to another, and this implied affirmation is in fact false.[2] And it may well be argued that the question 'Do all mermaids wear spectacles?' is of this kind. We would normally hesitate to answer either 'Yes' or 'No' to this—we would be more inclined to reply, 'Since mermaids do not exist, your question cannot arise.' But if a question 'cannot arise', any proposition which presents itself as an answer to that question lacks sense, or lacks at all events the kind of sense which makes it possible to characterise it as true or false.

This view of the matter has been propounded in recent years by Mr Strawson,[3] and Professor Passmore.[4] These writers differ from one another a little in their terminology and emphasis, and all express themselves with some deliberation. Professor Passmore, for example, is careful not to speak of 'true, false and meaningless propositions', but rather of *sentences* which express true propositions, false propositions and no proposition at all. If it be held that no sentence in which the subject-word is without application can express a proposition, then any four *propositions* of the forms 'Every X is Y', 'No X is Y', 'Some X is Y' and 'Some X is not Y' will

[1] *Logic*, pt. I, p. 139.
[2] *Elements*, III.9. Whately gives the 'hackneyed instance' of 'asking a man "whether he had *left off* beating his father",' and some less hackneyed ones.
[3] P. F. Strawson, 'On Referring', *Mind*, July 1950 (see, in particular, pp. 343–4).
[4] J. A. Passmore, 'Logical Positivism (I)', *Australasian Journal of Psychology and Philosophy*, Dec. 1943 (p. 82).

obey all the Aristotelian rules of opposition. But to preserve the rules of conversion and syllogism it must be added that sentences whose *predicate*-words are without application also fail to express propositions (for we cannot say that any proposition of the form 'No X is Y' entails the corresponding proposition of the form 'No Y is X', if the sentence 'No horses are dragons' is taken to express a proposition while 'No dragons are horses' does not). Still further extensions of the realm of the 'meaningless' would be necessary, in this system, to preserve inferences involving negative and complex terms.

One problem posed by the Strawson-Passmore point of view is this: If the question 'Do all mermaids wear spectacles?' just cannot arise because there are no mermaids, must not the same be said, for the same reason, of the question, 'Do mermaids exist?' But in that case we cannot even raise the question as to whether the question 'Do all mermaids wear spectacles?' can arise or not. This may be answered by arguing that the question 'Do mermaids exist?' is sensible only because it is not really about mermaids but about something else; and this answer may either be elaborated in the manner of Bain, by saying that its meaning is something like 'Do any women have tails like fish?', or in the manner of Lord Russell, by turning it into 'Is anything a mermaid?' The latter alternative cannot be taken if it is held that the predicate as well as the subject suggested by the question must have application for the question to make sense. But if we do take it, we obtain a curious result if we try to frame the question which the question 'Is anything a mermaid?' itself presupposes. This question must be 'Do *things* exist?', or 'Is anything a thing?', and this question in its turn can presuppose nothing but itself.

This brings us to a point at which the possibility of 'meaninglessness' is implicitly appealed to even in the system of *Principia Mathematica*. For in that system, the Aristotelian rules of opposition all hold if our square is constructed with the forms 'Everything is X', 'Nothing is X', 'Something is X', and Something is not X'.[1] And

---

[1] The subalternation of 'Something is XY' to 'Everything is XY' was implicitly recognised by Venn and Keynes, and that broadly on the ground given here. See the latter's *Formal Logic*, 4th ed., p. 226, n. 3. (See also Johnson's *Logical Calculus*, 1st article, §§11 and 14. I suspect that it was Johnson's article which converted Keynes to Venn's view on this point between his second and his third editions. See 2nd ed., p. 145, n. 1; 3rd ed., p. 191, n. 4.

the real reason for this—though not the one given in the text of *Principia Mathematica* itself[1]—is that in that system the possibility of universal propositions being verified by the non-existence of their subjects just cannot arise when the subject-term, if term it may be called, is the indefinite 'thing'. It cannot arise because the Russellian method of eliminating 'existence' as a genuine predicate involves treating 'thing' as the kind of term that can only function as a subject, so that the question 'Is anything a thing?' is senseless. Or we might use Frege's language and say that this question is senseless because in 'Something is X', etc., 'thing' does not signify a 'concept', of which we could ask whether anything falls under it, but rather the whole phrase 'Something is —' signifies a second-level concept under which we have placed the concept signified by 'X'.

What has just been said of the Aristotelian behaviour, even in the Russellian system, of the forms 'Everything is X', etc., suggests a presentation of some of the paradoxes of existential import which may make them appear a little less paradoxical. For in Lord Russell's view all A, E, I and O propositions are capable of being cast into the forms just mentioned. But when this is done with universals and particulars of the ordinary sort—'Every X is Y', etc.—it is found that they have different predicates. 'Every X is Y' turns into 'Everything is not-X-without-being-Y'; 'Some X is not Y' into 'Something is X-without-being-Y'; 'No X is Y' into 'Nothing is both-X-and-Y' (or 'Everything is not-both-X-and-Y') and 'Some X is Y' into 'Something is both-X-and-Y'. And there is nothing surprising in the fact that 'Everything is not-X-without-being-Y' should not imply 'Something is both-X-and-Y'—it is not that subalternation is invalid; the point is rather that these are not real subalterns. We cannot, however, reinstate the Aristotelian rules of conversion and syllogism in this manner, for the very fact which makes it possible to reinstate the rules of opposition is that our propositions are expressed with the kind of subject that cannot function also as a predicate. (With propositions of this sort the operation of conversion must be transferred from the subject and predicate to the components of the predicate; the convertibility of E and I, for example, amounting to the equivalence of the compound terms 'both X and Y' and 'both Y and X'.)

---

[1] For this, see the note on *24.52. There is a hint, though, of what I have called the 'real' reason in this note too.

4. *The existential import of singulars*

Aristotle, it will be recalled, argued in the *Categories* that if Socrates does not exist, then the proposition 'Socrates is not ill' is automatically true. But Keynes, in the brief section on the existential import of singulars which appears in his second[1] and third[2] editions (but is dropped from the fourth), argues that we would normally take both 'Socrates lived in Athens' and 'Socrates did not live in Athens' to be about a real person, and would tend to regard both as false if there were no such person. And as a consequence of this, he suggests that for the proper contradictory of 'Socrates lived in Athens' we must give the hypothetical form '*If* there was any such person as Socrates, he did not live in Athens'. On similar grounds, Johnson argues in his *Logic*[3] that to deny 'S is P', where 'S' is a singular subject, we should say 'Either S is not or S is not P', and to deny 'S is not P' we should say 'Either S is not or S is P'. There is an obvious clumsiness about this, but there is a real enough difficulty behind it. The difficulty, and the possible methods of solving it, were very thoroughly canvassed in a controversy between Professor C. H. Langford and J. A. Chadwick which ran through the pages of *Mind* from 1927 to 1929,[4] and which Professor E. J. Nelson re-opened in 1946.[5]

The positions of these three writers may be summed up in three opponent syllogisms. Professor Langford's argument in effect runs

> No pair of propositions in which both members presuppose the existence of their subject is a pair of contradictories;
> But any pair of singulars is a pair of propositions in which both members presuppose the existence of their subject;
> Therefore no pair of singulars is a pair of contradictories.

The opponent syllogism implicit in Chadwick's argument runs

[1] §107.

[2] §123.

[3] I.v.3–5.

[4] C. H. Langford, 'On Propositions Belonging to Logic', *Mind* 1927; J. A. Chadwick, ibid., 1927; C. H. Langford, 'Singular Propositions', ibid., 1928; J. A. Chadwick, ibid., 1928; C. H. Langford, 'Propositions Directly About Particulars', ibid., 1929.

[5] E. J. Nelson, 'Contradiction and the presupposition of existence', *Mind* 1946. (The controversy has dragged on further since.)

No pair of propositions in which both members presuppose the
existence of their subject is a pair of contradictories;
But some pairs of singulars are pairs of contradictories;
Therefore some pairs of singulars are not pairs in which both
members presuppose the existence of their subject.

To support this conclusion, Chadwick distinguishes 'It is not the
case that this has roundness' from 'This lacks roundness', and 'This
has roundness' from 'It is not the case that this lacks roundness',
arguing that both the shorter forms imply 'This exists', while the
longer forms do not; and he suggests that this is the solution that
Keynes and Johnson are feeling after in the passages just cited.
Among the objections which Professor Langford raises is one to the
effect that if you can do this sort of thing with 'This is round' you
ought to be able to do it with 'This exists', but it seems absurd to
say that there is a sense of 'This exists' (namely 'It is not the case
that this lacks existence') in which it could be true even if the 'This'
in question did not exist. The third opponent syllogism, that
implicit in Professor Nelson's contribution, runs

Any pair of singulars is a pair of contradictories in which both
members presuppose the existence of their subject;
And some pairs of singulars are pairs of contradictories;
Therefore some pairs of propositions in which both members
presuppose the existence of their subject are pairs of contradictories.

To meet the objection that this presupposition of existence makes
it possible for both members of any such pair to be false, Professor
Nelson distinguishes between 'presupposing' and 'implying' (it is
in fact Professor Nelson who introduces the word 'presuppose' into
this discussion—the others simply say 'imply'). He says that for a
proposition to be true it is necessary that anything that it implies
should be true; but that what it 'presupposes' should be true is
necessary not only to its truth but to its very existence. If the subject
of 'This is round' did not exist, that proposition would not be false,
for there could not in that case be any such proposition.

If Chadwick echoes the Johnson of the *Logic*, Professor Nelson
echoes the Johnson of *The Logical Calculus*,[1] where it is argued that

[1] II, 14.

5

'the "existence" of a subject is . . . a presupposition of significant judgment'. The difference between the earlier and the later Johnson at this point is not, however, as great as it may seem. In the *Logic*, where singulars of the form 'S is not' are contemplated, it seems to be understood that the subject-term is a descriptive singular name like 'The number 3' or 'The integer between 4 and 5'. But in *The Logical Calculus* Johnson is speaking primarily of singular propositions with 'purely denotative names' for their subject-terms, and no word functions as a 'name' in this sense until it has been attached to some actual object. Secondarily he is speaking of universal and particular propositions, the significance of which presupposes what he calls a 'universe of denotation'—a *set* of real objects of which we can say, e.g. that any one of them that is X is Y, or (what comes to the same thing) that none of them is X without being Y. The extension to words like 'This' of the doctrine laid down in the *Logic* for expressions like 'The integer between 4 and 5' seems to be Chadwick's idea, not Johnson's.

A sharp distinction between the case of 'purely denotative' singular names and that of 'definite descriptions' is characteristic of the Russellian logic in its best-known phase, though in his later years Lord Russell has toyed with the idea of eliminating names of the former sort. The Russellian view, as we have indicated earlier, is not merely that propositions of the form 'This is Y' and 'This is not Y' are meaningless if 'This' does not denote anything, but that the forms 'This exists' and 'This does not exist' are meaningless whether 'This' denotes anything or not, so long as it is a purely denotative word: 'existence' can only be significantly affirmed or denied, on the Russellian view, where the subject is indicated by a descriptive expression, and then it means that the description has or has not application. The fact that we can intelligibly raise the question as to whether or not there was any such person as Homer or Socrates simply shows, in Lord Russell's view, that these are only 'grammatical' and not 'logical' proper names—the meaning they have for us does not lie in their direct reference to some individual who has been pointed out to us, but in some feature of these individuals which they 'connote' for us. 'Homer', for example, might mean 'the person called "Homer" who wrote the *Iliad*', and 'Homer did not exist' that there was never any person answering to this description (the *Iliad* having been written by several people or by someone not called 'Homer'). This connotation may not be clearly fixed by any general convention, but it is only because of it that we can use these names intelligibly at all, though they may have been genuine proper names in the hands of those who were acquainted with the individuals in question. The true 'logical proper names' are demonstratives.[1]

In the case of 'definite descriptions', i.e. most phrases beginning with 'The' (and, as we have just seen, most grammatical proper names), the existence of the subject is on the Russellian view part of the meaning of the expression. 'The King of France is bald' means 'There *is* at least one King of France, and not more than one, and he is bald'. Hence any sentence introduced by a definite description which has no application is *ipso facto* false. We might illustrate this point of view by considering a celebrated sentence in Whately's *Elements*:[2] 'The Organon (1) of Bacon (2) was not designed (3) to supersede (4) the Organon (5) of Aristotle (6).' Whately says that if we put the emphasis on each numbered word we obtain six different propositions (he means primarily six different ways of dividing the sentence into subject and predicate), but that 'each of them implies the truth of all the rest'. But if we set out these six propositions in a manner which makes explicit the differences which Whately intended, thus:

(1) The work of Bacon's which was designed to supersede the Organon of Aristotle was not his own *Organon*;
(2) The author whose Organon was designed to supersede the Organon of Aristotle was not *Bacon*;
(3) The manner in which Bacon's Organon superseded the Organon of Aristotle was not *by design*;
(4) The relation which Bacon intended his Organon to have to the Organon of Aristotle was not that of *superseding* it;
(5) The work of Aristotle's which Bacon's Organon was designed to supersede was not the former's *Organon*; and
(6) The author whose Organon Bacon's was designed to supersede was not *Aristotle*;

we see that each of them implies the existence of something the

[1] *Principia Mathematica*, note on *14.21; *The Problems of Philosophy*, ch. 5.
[2] II.iv.1.

existence of which is not implied by any of the others, so that their truth-conditions are not quite identical.

With negations, however, Lord Russell makes a distinction. If 'The (present) King of France is not bald' is regarded as predicating '— is not bald' of 'The King of France', then it means 'There is at least one King of France, and not more than one, and he is not bald', and is false because there is no King of France. But if it just means 'It is not the case that the King of France is bald' then it is true for the same reason. (It then means the simple contradictory of 'The King of France is bald', i.e. it means 'Either there is no King of France, or there is more than one King of France, or the one King of France has some hair', and is true because the first alternative is realised.)[1] With descriptions, in other words, Lord Russell admits Chadwick's two kinds of negation.

One consequence of the Russellian view that 'This exists' and 'This does not exist' are meaningless is that such sentences as 'This could not but exist' and 'This might not have existed' are also meaningless. Of any directly denoted object, we can intelligibly say that its characteristics might have been different from what they in fact are—we can say, e.g. 'This, which is in fact red, might have been not red but blue', but we cannot intelligibly say 'This might not have existed'. This consequence of the Russellian view has been drawn, and accepted, by Wittgenstein,[2] Ramsey[3] and Professor Broad.[4] Professor Moore, on the other hand, regards it as a reason for rejecting this part of the Russellian system.[5] He admits that when we say 'Lions exist' the 'existence' of which we are speaking cannot be intelligibly predicated of a bare 'This'; but he argues that there must be some other sense of the word in which 'This exists' is intelligible, because 'This might not have existed' is not only intelligible but in most cases true. (He further admits that 'This exists' is a queer sort of proposition inasmuch as we could not frame

---

[1] *Principia Mathematica*, Introduction to 1st edition, ch. 3; *Introduction to Mathematical Philosophy*, p. 179.

[2] *Tractatus Logico-Philosophicus*, 2.022, 2.023.

[3] *The Foundations of Mathematics*, pp. 285; 59–61; 154–5.

[4] *Examination of McTaggart's Philosophy*, vol. 1, pp. 252–64.

[5] *Is Existence a Predicate?*, Arist. Soc. Supp. Vol. XV (1936), pp. 186–8. For a similar criticism of Lord Russell, and also of the part of Lord Russell's theory which Professor Moore accepts, see J. N. Findlay, *Meinong's Theory of Objects*, pp. 53–4.

it if it were not true, and similarly we could not frame the proposition 'This does not exist' if it were not in fact false.)[1]

This dispute has theological bearings. Lord Russell has noted that his account of 'existence' makes the ontological argument for the existence of God fallacious; but he has not noted that it equally invalidates the 'cosmological' argument or argument *a contingentia mundi*. This is the argument that if a thing exists when it might equally well not have existed, the realisation of one rather than the other of these two possibilities requires a cause, and the ultimate cause must be a Being which could not but have existed, i.e. a Necessary Being or God; and there obviously *are* things which exist when they might equally well not have existed; *ergo*, etc. But on the Russellian view 'might not have existed' means nothing unless it is a roundabout way of saying that something might have been different in character. We might say that this view replaces the old belief in a single Necessary Being by the belief that anything whatever is a 'necessary being', in the sense that the assertion that it might not have existed is meaningless. Professor Moore in effect restores one of the premises of the cosmological argument to significance.

If Professor Moore objects to Lord Russell's contention that 'This does not exist' is not false but meaningless, there are others who have objected to his view that 'The King of France is not bald' is not meaningless but false. Attempts have been made, particularly by Mr Strawson,[2] to rehabilitate (with modifications) a theory of Frege's on the subject which Lord Russell thought of his own theory as superseding. To understand Frege's position, it is necessary to turn again to his theory that sentences 'express' propositions and 'denote' truth-values. The 'sense' of a sentence, i.e. what proposition it expresses, depends in part upon the 'sense' of its subject-term. Thus 'The morning star is a planet' and 'The evening star is a planet' express different propositions, because the phrase 'The morning star' expresses a different 'sense' from the phrase 'The evening star', though they both denote Venus. The denotation of a

---

[1] To say 'This does not exist' is rather like answering 'No' to the telephonist's question, 'Are you there?' (I owe this comparison to my wife.)

[2] 'On referring', *Mind* 1950. This title indicates that the article is intended as a reconsideration of the matters dealt with in Lord Russell's article 'On denoting' in *Mind* 1905, in which his characteristic theories about 'the King of France' were first put forward. (This article has been reprinted in Feigl and Sellars's *Readings in Philosophical Analysis*.)

sentence, on the other hand—that is, its truth or falsity—does not depend on the sense, but only on the denotation of its subject-term. Thus 'The morning star is a planet' will continue to denote the True if any other word or phrase denoting Venus is substituted for 'The morning star'.

Certain difficulties arise here, however, in connection with such a sentence as 'That the morning star is a planet is believed by Mr Pinkerton', where the subject is itself a sentence and so would appear to denote a truth-value. For even if Mr Pinkerton does in fact believe this, if we replace the subject by another sentence denoting the same truth-value, e.g. by the sentence 'The sum of the first n odd numbers is equal to n^2' (which, like 'The morning star is a planet', denotes the True), we have no guarantee that this also will be among the beliefs of Mr Pinkerton, i.e. that the sentence as a whole will 'denote the True' as the original sentence did. Frege's solution of this is that sentences occurring as subordinate clauses do not always have the same denotation as when they occur independently, but often denote the proposition which in their ordinary use they do not 'denote' but 'express'. This is so in such cases as the above, where the truth-value of 'That the morning star is a planet is believed by Mr Pinkerton' will remain unaltered if the subject is replaced by another sentence which, used independently, would express the same proposition as 'The morning star is a planet', used independently, would express. (There are some cases in which subordinate clauses do denote truth-values, namely when the sentence as a whole is a 'truth-function' of the clause in question. For example, in 'The morning star is a planet and 2 and 2 are 4', the whole will continue to denote the True if 'The morning star is a planet' is replaced by any other true proposition.) From this dependence of the denotation of a sentence upon the denotation of its subject-term, it follows as a corollary that where the subject-term does not denote anything at all, as in 'The King of France is bald', the sentence as a whole does not denote anything at all, i.e. is neither true nor false; though so long as the subject-term has a 'sense' the sentence also has a 'sense', and is to that extent not 'meaningless'.[1]

These will suffice as illustrations of positions that have been taken up on the question as to the existential import of singulars.

[1] These aspects of Frege's thought are developed in his paper 'On sense and reference'.

I have no decision of my own to record on this very difficult topic; but something should be added about a class of singulars to which not much attention has been paid in these disputes, namely singulars beginning with such phrases as 'This man', 'This tree', etc. They are of some importance because if it be contended that, say, 'Every mermaid wears spectacles' does not imply 'Some mermaid wears spectacles' (since the latter implies that something is a mermaid while the former does not), it may well be asked. 'But does not "Every mermaid wears spectacles" imply "*This* mermaid wears spectacles"? and does not "This mermaid wears spectacles" imply "Some mermaid wears spectacles"? And is not a consequence of a consequence of a proposition itself a consequence of that proposition?' The point to be decided about 'This X is Y' is not so much whether it is true or false when 'This' is not being used to denote anything, but whether it is true or false when what it denotes is not an X. What is the truth-value of 'This mermaid wears spectacles', when what I am pointing to is indeed wearing spectacles, but is not a mermaid? Here again it may be argued that until it is established that the object indicated is a mermaid, the question as to whether 'this mermaid' wears spectacles 'cannot arise'; but if we are not satisfied with this we must say, I think, that the phrase 'This mermaid' is ambiguous. It may mean 'This is a mermaid, and it . . .', or it may mean 'If this is a mermaid, then it . . .'. It is only in the sense of 'If this is a mermaid it wears spectacles' that 'This mermaid wears spectacles' follows from 'Every mermaid wears spectacles' (interpreted in the manner of Brentano and Venn); but if this is what it means, 'Some mermaid wears spectacles' does not follow from it. 'Some mermaid wears spectacles' does follow from it if it means 'This is a mermaid and it wears spectacles'; but in this sense it does not itself follow from 'Every mermaid wears spectacles', either in the Brentano-Venn sense or in any other sense that has been seriously put forward.

APPENDIX

The Contents of 'The Craft of Formal Logic'

Index

accidents, 67, 69

adjectives, 57

affirmation, 13, 14, 15; universal, 43; of negative terms, 54

analytic judgements, 76–7, 81–2

Apuleius, 15, 40

Aristotle, 13, 14, 15, 26, 28, 37–8, 42ff., 49ff., 59, 60, 61, 64, 66ff., 70, 83n., 103, 104, 123, 128

article, indefinite, 42–3

attributes, 62, 67; classes of, 62, 63; essential, 69, 73. *See* connotation

Bain, A., 79, 85, 114–16

belief, 18ff., ascriptive theory of, 26ff., 51

Black, M., 90n., 98n.

Bochenski, I. M., 15n.

Boethius, 40

Bolzano, B., 19, 30, 32

Boole, G., 117, 118

Bradley, 77, 82n., 87

Brentano, F., 22–3, 111ff., 118, 122–3, 135

Broad, C. D., 21, 23, 32n., 36n., 82n., 87, 101n., 132

Brown, T., 75, 76

Carnap, R., 104

categoricals, logic of, 89

categories, 64–6, 76, 103

Chadwick, J. A., 128–30

classes, 68, 70–2, 74, 93–5; classes of all classes, 94–5; null classes, 93, 124; unit class, 93

Coffey, P., 38n., 58n.

commas, inverted, 104–5

concepts, first and second order, 91–2

Conceptualists, 100

connotation, of terms, 72–3; of names, 73; conventional, 81

consequences, formal and material, 51

Contradiction, Law of, 41

contradictions, 46–7

contraries, 43–4, 46

Cook Wilson, J. A., 21, 25, 84n., 101

copula, 49, 54–6, 86ff. *See also* 'is'

Couturat, L., 117

cosmological argument, 133

Craft of Formal Logic, The, contents of, 136–9

Demos, R., 54n.

definition, ostensive, 81

denial, 13, 16, 40ff., 43ff., 54

denotation, 72, 133–4

Descartes, R., 114

descriptions, definite, 74, 96ff., 131ff.

determinables, 63–4, 84

essence, 67–8, 76

Excluded Middle, Law of, 41

existence, intentional, 22; not a predicate?, 113–14

extension, conventional, or exemplification, 80–1

facts, 23ff.

False, the, 98

Findlay, J. N., 20n., 26n., 28n., 39n., 132n.

Flew, A. G. N., 39n.